The People's Bible Teachings

ANGELS AND DEMONS

Have Wings—Will Travel

John D. Schuetze

NORTHWESTERN PUBLISHING HOUSE
Milwaukee, Wisconsin

Second printing, 1998

Library of Congress Card 96-71904
Northwestern Publishing House
1250 N. 113th St., Milwaukee, WI 53226-3284
© 1997 by Northwestern Publishing House.
Published 1997
Printed in the United States of America
ISBN 0-8100-0684-7

Table of Contents

Let your holy angel be with me,
that the wicked foe may have
no power over me.

Luther's Morning Prayer

Editor's Preface

The People's Bible Teachings is a series of books on all of the main doctrinal teachings of the Bible.

Following the pattern set by The People's Bible series, these books are written especially for laypeople. Theological terms, when used, are explained in everyday language so that people can understand them. The authors show how Christian doctrine is drawn directly from clear passages of Scripture and then how those doctrines apply to people's faith and life. Most importantly, these books show how every teaching of Scripture points to Christ, our only Savior.

The authors of The People's Bible Teachings are parish pastors and professors who have had years of experience teaching the Bible. They are men of scholarship and practical insight.

We take this opportunity to express our gratitude to Professor Leroy Dobberstein of Wisconsin Lutheran Seminary, Mequon, Wisconsin, and Professor Thomas Nass of Martin Luther College, New Ulm, Minnesota, for serving as consultants for this series. Their insights and assistance have been invaluable.

We pray that the Lord will use these volumes to help his people grow in their faith, knowledge, and understanding of his saving teachings, which he has revealed to us in the Bible. To God alone be the glory.

Curtis A. Jahn
Series Editor

Introduction

Good versus evil. This conflict has been part of the universe ever since Satan rebelled against God, and it only intensified with the fall into sin. This struggle is not only evident in the material world where we live. It is being waged in the spirit world as well.

One of the most common pictures of good versus evil is found in the Wild West. There we find lawman and outlaw, hero and villain engaged in a constant struggle of good versus evil. Whether we acted out this conflict in a childhood game of "cops and robbers" or watched it being played out in a TV western, the unwritten rule was that the good guys would always win.

This rule becomes reality in the world of angels and demons. Although the forces are strong and the fighting is fierce, good will eventually win. That's a victory God predicted in Eden and a truth Jesus impressed upon his disciples. He assured them that his church was built on a rock that the gates of hell would not overcome (Matthew 16:18).

We want to remember this truth as we enter the world of angels and demons. As in any war, the scenes will get ugly at times, especially those that deal with the devil. Yet we can view this war knowing that good will prevail over evil. For this isn't just a battle between angels and demons, but between God and Satan. It's a battle that Jesus fought—and won—on the cross.

Jesus said, "It is finished." With that,
he bowed his head and gave up his spirit.
John 19:30

1

The Creation of the Angels

A Posse Is Formed

The state of Texas has long boasted about its size. Its wide-open spaces were a nightmare for lawmen back in the 1800s. With so much open space for lawbreakers to roam, lawmen had a difficult time trying to enforce the law everywhere. To meet this challenge the Texas Rangers were organized. This group soon grew into a regiment of five hundred men who worked at keeping law and order in the land.

God also has a group of rangers—the angels. Like a large posse, they serve the Sheriff of heaven and earth. And their work is not confined to the state of Texas.

Though they are rarely seen, these invisible rangers roam the earth as they serve their heavenly Master.

Time of creation

In 1823 Stephen F. Austin formed a band of mounted riflemen. At first his goal was only to protect American settlers along the Brazos River. Twelve years later the members of this group formally organized as the Texas Rangers, and for many years they enforced the law for the entire state.

Exactly when and where God created his "rangers" isn't quite so clear. Only indirectly does Scripture tell us the angels were created during the six days of creation. Exodus 20:11 states, "For in six days the LORD made the heavens and the earth, the sea, and all that is in them." The "all" in this verse would include the angels. They are not from eternity but were created by God. Paul told the Colossians, "By [Christ] all things were created: things in heaven and on earth, visible and invisible" (1:16). The invisible creatures in heaven are the angels. In speaking about the angels, the psalm writer states, "[God] commanded and they were created" (Psalm 148:5).

As with the rest of his creatures, God made the angels during the six days of creation. However, pinpointing the day he did this is difficult. A careful reading of Genesis 1 and 2 offers little help. While we know God created light on the first day and human beings on the sixth day, angels are not mentioned. The first reference to them in Scripture is after the fall. Genesis 3:24 tells us God sent some of his rangers (here called cherubim) to "guard the way to the tree of life."

Although Genesis 1 doesn't tell us on which day the angels were created, the book of Job may shed some light on the subject. Toward the end of the book the Lord asks Job, "Where were you when I laid the earth's foundation? Tell me, if you understand. Who marked off its dimensions? Surely you know! Who stretched a measuring line across it? On what were its footings set, or who laid its cornerstone—while the morning stars sang together and all the angels shouted for joy?" (38:4-7).

This passage seems to indicate that the angels witnessed the world's creation. If this is the case, these words in Job would suggest that God made the angels early in the creation process, that they were there when God called the world into existence out of nothing, and that they observed it as it took shape and became filled with life at the Lord's command. Yet it would be difficult to establish this with absolute certainty on the basis of so little evidence. At any rate, the important thing is not when angels were created, but that we recognize them as real beings, not mere mythological creatures.

Size of God's force

Unlike the human population of the world, the number of the angels remains constant. Jesus told some of his critics, "Those who are considered worthy of taking part in that age and in the resurrection from the dead will neither marry nor be given in marriage, and they can no longer die; for they are like the angels" (Luke 20:35,36).

Will we become angels when we die? That is a common misconception. The typical stereotype of heaven shows people wearing wings and halos, floating around on clouds and playing harps. But notice, that's not what Jesus said. We will not become angels when we die. We won't join God's rangers. In heaven we will wear a crown, not a badge.

Yet we will be like angels in two ways: angels are eternal and they don't marry. Since they don't have families, their number doesn't increase. And since they don't die, their number doesn't decrease either. It remains constant.

This number is very large. Daniel 7:10 puts the force at "ten thousand times ten thousand." Jesus told Peter he could immediately muster an army of more than 12 legions (Matthew 26:53). Since a single legion was around six thousand, this was quite an army of angels who were ready to serve the Savior. The writer of Hebrews describes what we might call the Lord's guardians at heaven's gates: "But you have come to Mount Zion, to the heavenly Jerusalem, the city of the living God. You have come to thousands upon thousands of angels in joyful assembly" (12:22). All these passages indicate that God created a countless number of angels.

Spiritual beings

The number of the angels is great. Yet each one is a distinct being and not just part of a large impersonal force. Some are even given names in Scripture. An angel named Gabriel appeared on four different occasions—twice to the prophet Daniel (Daniel 8:16; 9:21) and once each to Zechariah (Luke 1:19) and Mary (Luke 1:26). The other angel we know by name is Michael (Jude 9; Revelation 12:7). Both of these angels, it would seem, hold important positions in God's regiment of rangers.

Scripture reveals that angels are spirits—without flesh and blood—as Hebrews 1:14 states: "Are not all angels ministering spirits sent to serve those who will inherit salvation?" As spirits, angels do not take up space, nor are they bound by time and space as we are in this world. This doesn't mean, however, that they are present everywhere. They are not like the Lord, who says, "Do not I fill heaven and earth?" (Jeremiah 23:24). Rather, though they do not take up space, they are confined to one place at any given moment.

Even though they are invisible, angels have the power to assume a visible form. Sometimes they appeared as ordinary people. For example, when the Lord sent two angels to rescue Lot from Sodom, they looked like ordinary men. Neither Lot nor the men of the city suspected they were angels. To accomplish their goal these heavenly rangers had gone "undercover." They concealed their identity by assuming human form (Genesis 19:1-5). Before this incident these same two angels had accompanied the Lord, who also assumed a human form, when he visited Abraham and Sarah (Genesis 18). Hebrews 13:2 probably refers to such incidents: "Do not forget to entertain strangers, for by so doing some people have entertained angels without knowing it."

At other times angels have appeared in full uniform. The shepherds witnessed such a display the night of Jesus' birth (Luke 2:9-14). This same brilliance was visible at Jesus' empty tomb on Easter. When the angel came to roll back the stone, Matthew tells us, "His appearance was like lightning, and his clothes were white as snow" (28:3). In each case the angels' appearance was brilliant. This brilliant appearance not only reflected their holiness but also the holiness of God, who sent them.

When we see pictures or statues of angels, they usually have wings. Whether angels regularly wore wings when they appeared to people, we don't know. Yet the Bible supports the idea that they have wings.

Artists usually portray angels with two wings, similar to the angels Solomon made for the temple (1 Kings 6:24). It appears that the angels placed on the ark of the covenant also had two wings (Exodus 25:20). The Bible often pictures angels with more than two wings, however. The seraphs Isaiah saw had six wings (Isaiah 6:2). The same was true for the angels John witnessed in a vision (Revelation 4:8). The angels Ezekiel describes have only four wings (Ezekiel 1:6). We will say more about the significance of the wings later.

Superior skills

The Texas Rangers often got their man as a result of quick thinking rather than force. Superior intellect is also characteristic of God's rangers. The angel Gabriel told Daniel, "I have now come to give you insight and understanding" (Daniel 9:22). Angels' intellects are superior to that of humans.

Even though much of this superior wisdom is given to them by God, some of it also comes through the preaching and teaching of the gospel, which takes place in God's church. Paul states that through the church the angels know "the manifold wisdom of God" (Ephesians 3:10). First Peter 1:12 adds that the angels welcomed the message of the Old Testament prophets, hoping to gain more insight and understanding into God's saving plan for his people on earth. This shows that angels are not only teachers but also students of God's truth. Just as some people "have entertained angels without knowing it" (Hebrews 13:2), so we can only wonder how many angels are present with us in church during worship without us realizing it (1 Corinthians 11:10). Think of that the next time you are in church. The empty place in the pew next to you may be filled by an angel eager to learn more about God's will for the world.

This superior wisdom of the angels, however, is not equal to that of God. As creatures they are inferior to their Creator. They are wise, but not all-knowing. In speaking about the end of the world Jesus refers to the limits of their knowledge: "No one knows about that day or hour, not even the angels in heaven" (Matthew 24:36). The abilities of the angels are nothing when compared to God, whose wisdom and power are limitless.

While the power of angels is inferior to that of God, it is superior to our human abilities. As God's rangers they are quick on the draw and would beat us every time in a contest of skills. In Psalm 8 David writes, "What is man that you are mindful of him, the son of man that you care for him? You made him a little lower than the heavenly beings" (verses 4,5). Here David tells us that angels have abilities superior to that of us human beings. Elsewhere he refers to them as "mighty ones who do [God's] bidding" (Psalm 103:20). Paul used the word "powerful" to describe them (2 Thessalonians 1:7). It's comforting to know such an impressive force is on our side.

When Psalm 8:4 says that God made the "son of man" a "little lower than the heavenly beings," it is not only referring to the creation of the human race, but also to Jesus in his state of humiliation. Jesus placed himself below the angels and even accepted help from these heavenly beings, such as after his temptations (Matthew 4:11) and in the Garden of Gethsemane (Luke 22:43). He accepted this humble position as part of his work of winning a place in heaven for us.

Different ranks

As in any law enforcement agency, there are also different ranks among God's rangers. God sent cherubim to guard Eden's gate (Genesis 3:24). Isaiah encountered seraphs during his close encounter with God (Isaiah 6:2). Looking ahead to the Last Day, Paul speaks of "the voice of the archangel and . . . the trumpet call of God" (1 Thessalonians 4:16).

The term *archangel* means "chief angel." In Daniel 10:13 the prophet calls the archangel Michael "one of the chief princes." From this passage it is hard to determine whether Michael is the only archangel or one of several. As the archangel he could be the head of God's inner cabinet of angels who are superior to other angels in rank and power. Or he could be the chief of all angels, second only to God in power. This latter thought is supported by the fact that the Bible never speaks of more than one archangel. The word always appears in the singular (1 Thessalonians 4:16; Jude 9). On the basis of Scripture, however, this remains an open question. There could be a single archangel, or there could be several.

Another class of angels mentioned quite often in the Bible is the cherubim. Ezekiel describes them in some detail:

> In the fire was what looked like four living creatures. In appearance their form was that of a man, but each of them had four faces and four wings. Their legs were straight; their feet were like those of a calf and gleamed like burnished bronze. Under their wings on their four sides they had the hands of a man. All four of them had faces and wings, and their wings touched one another. Each one went straight ahead; they did not turn as they moved.

> Their faces looked like this: Each of the four had the face of a man, and on the right side each had the face of a lion, and on the left the face of an ox; each also had the face of an eagle. Such were their faces. Their wings were spread

out upward; each had two wings, one touching the wing of another creature on either side, and two wings covering its body. Each one went straight ahead. Wherever the spirit would go, they would go, without turning as they went. The appearance of the living creatures was like burning coals of fire or like torches. Fire moved back and forth among the creatures; it was bright, and lightning flashed out of it. The creatures sped back and forth like flashes of lightning (1:5-14).

At first Ezekiel didn't know these creatures were angels. It wasn't until he saw them in a later vision that he confessed, "These were the living creatures I had seen beneath the God of Israel by the Kebar River, and I realized that they were cherubim" (10:20).

The apostle John also saw four living creatures in a vision he records in Revelation 4. They are similar to those that Ezekiel observed, yet they do not match up in every respect. John speaks of six wings; Ezekiel mentions only four. John saw a different face on each of the four creatures; Ezekiel gives them each a four-sided face. In both Ezekiel and John the four faces are those of a man, lion, ox, and eagle. In spite of the differences, it is quite likely John observed the same cherubim that Ezekiel saw centuries earlier. Since angels are spirits, they can assume different forms at different times, whether on earth or in heaven.

On the basis of these accounts, it appears that the four cherubim serve as honor guards before the throne of God. The description of the ark of the covenant in the Old Testament reflects this relationship between the Lord and the cherubim. The ark is described as "the ark of the covenant of the LORD Almighty, who is enthroned between the cherubim" (1 Samuel 4:4; see also Exodus 25:22; 2 Samuel

6:2). Several of the psalms also speak this way. In Psalm 80 Asaph prays, "Hear us, O Shepherd of Israel, you who lead Joseph like a flock; you who sit enthroned between the cherubim, shine forth" (verse 1). Hezekiah also addressed God as the one "enthroned between the cherubim" when he spoke to him in prayer (Isaiah 37:16).

Seraphs (also called seraphim in the plural) are another class of angels mentioned in the Bible. In Isaiah 6:2 we are told, "Above him were seraphs, each with six wings: With two wings they covered their faces, with two they covered their feet, and with two they were flying." It is difficult to determine the significance of the various positions of their wings. The fact that they use their wings to cover themselves in God's presence may signify the humility that even the angels feel in God's majestic and holy presence.

Scripture also seems to refer to various ranks of angels when it describes them as "thrones or powers or rulers or authorities" (Colossians 1:16; see also Ephesians 3:10; 6:12 for similar ranks of angels).

Even though angels differ in rank, their mission is the same. Their task is to serve God and carry out his will.

Confirmed in holiness

What God said about the rest of his creation was also true of angels. They were made "very good." God created them perfect and holy.

Yet not all the angels stayed in this state of perfection. Shortly after their creation some angels sinned against God. In this respect they were much like Adam and Eve. They were created holy, but they could sin. Some of them did. They rebelled against God. Later their leader in the rebellion, Satan, brought about the fall of man.

However, not all the angels joined Satan in his evil endeavor. Some remained loyal to their loving God. In love their gracious Creator confirmed these loyal messengers in their holiness, so that they are no longer able to fall into sin as did Satan and the other angels who joined him. Just as we will be confirmed in holiness in heaven and will not even be able to sin anymore, so the holy angels have been forever confirmed in holiness. Paul's reference to the "elect angels" (1 Timothy 5:21) would support this truth. Certainly their election is much different from that of believers. They were not elected because of Christ's atoning work. Jesus didn't die to save the good angels, for they never sinned (Hebrews 2:16). Rather, with the phrase "elect angels" Paul is stressing that by God's grace these good angels were confirmed in their holiness.

In other places also Scripture speaks indirectly about the good angels being confirmed in holiness. In Luke 20:36 Jesus says that the good angels can never die, implying that it is no longer possible for them ever to fall into sin. In Matthew 18:10 Jesus states that God's angels always see his face, again implying that their state of holiness will never change.

As believers in Christ, we can look forward to this same "confirmation ceremony" in heaven. We too will be confirmed in holiness. We will be holy, and we will not be able to sin. And together with the angels we will live in God's glory forever.

2

The Ministry of the Angels

God's Pony Express

Did you ever wonder what it would be like to be an angel? Not only do they fly from place to place with amazing speed, they also have an important ministry to carry out. That ministry is to serve God.

The first way they serve their Creator is by worshiping him. This worship began at creation. Job 38:7 tells us that when God laid the earth's foundation, "all the angels shouted for joy."

This worship has continued through time. The prophet Isaiah witnessed the heavenly chorus singing the responsive song "Holy, holy, holy is the LORD Almighty; the whole earth is full of his glory" (Isaiah 6:3). This celestial choir was so powerful the prophet adds, "At the sound of their voices the doorposts and thresholds shook" (verse 4).

This worship will continue throughout eternity. In Revelation John describes several concerts put on by the angelic choir in which they join in that beautiful song: "Praise and glory and wisdom and thanks and honor and power and strength be to our God for ever and ever. Amen!" (7:12). Together with the saints in heaven and on earth, these divine servants hold a continual worship service to the glory of God.

Divine messengers

Angels, however, don't serve God only by worshiping him and singing his praises. They also serve God in other ways, as the name *angel* indicates. It means "messenger." Drawing another illustration from the Wild West, we could call the angels "God's Pony Express." This is a fitting analogy since in several cases the Bible refers to angels as "horses and chariots of fire." This is what Elisha's servant observed when the Lord enabled him to see the large angelic army that was protecting Elisha and him (2 Kings 6:17). Earlier it was "a chariot of fire and horses of fire" (2 Kings 2:11) that carried Elijah to heaven. When we recall that angels carried Lazarus to Abraham's side (Luke 16:22), we find more support identifying these fiery horses and chariots as angels.

The prophet Zechariah pictures angels in a similar way. He relates:

> During the night I had a vision—and there before me was a man riding a red horse! He was standing among the myrtle trees in a ravine. Behind him were red, brown and white horses.

I asked, "What are these, my lord?"

The angel who was talking with me answered, "I will show you what they are." Then the man standing among the myrtle trees explained, "They are the ones the LORD has sent to go throughout the earth" (Zechariah 1:8-10).

Just as Satan and his evil angels roam throughout the earth and go back and forth in it (Job 1:7), the holy angels do the same. As divine messengers they have often delivered mail to God's people on earth.

In the early 1860s the Pony Express ran between Missouri and California. Riders often averaged 250 miles a day as they traveled through rugged and dangerous terrain. They were there to deliver the mail. Only once was it lost, even though the riders compiled over 650,000 miles during the 18 months they ran the route.

The angels have a similar task. They not only police the world and protect God's people, they also deliver the mail. They were kept especially busy delivering mail during the time of Christ. They were "caught up in the Christmas rush," bringing divine messages to Zechariah, Mary, and Joseph, as well as the shepherds. It was an angel who warned Joseph to take his family to Egypt (Matthew 2:13), and it was an angel who told him when it was safe to return to the land of Israel (verse 19). To several surprised women an angel brought the Easter greeting "He is not here; he has risen" (Matthew 28:6). When Jesus ascended into heaven, an angel told some startled disciples, "This same Jesus, who has been taken from you into heaven, will come back in the same way you have seen him go into heaven" (Acts 1:11). As God's Pony Express the angels have made quite a few runs delivering the Master's message to his people on earth.

And their record is better than the Pony Express. They never lost the mail even once.

Priority mail

The Pony Express lasted only a short time. It was soon replaced by the telegraph, which could transmit a message much faster than a man on a horse. The same could be said for God's Pony Express. While the Lord can still send his heavenly messengers to deliver a divine message today, we should not expect this special service.

Instead of sending his message special delivery, God now uses bulk mailing. He has given us his Word in the Scriptures. There he delivers the most important message of all. John 20:31 tells us, "These are written that you may believe that Jesus is the Christ, the Son of God, and that by believing you may have life in his name." God has sent us all the spiritual information we need in his written Word. God's Word assures us that we have eternal life through faith in Christ and that one day Jesus will return and take us to our heavenly home. Until that time comes, we shouldn't expect to see angels delivering a divine message. God used them at special times in history to bring a specific message about his plan of salvation. Since this plan has now been carried out, the angels' role in this area seems to have ended. Just as the power to do miracles often accompanied a new revelation, so angels were often the ones to reveal a message. Just as the Lord has not promised us the power to do miracles, so he has not promised to communicate with us through angels. Rather, "faith comes from hearing the message, and the message is heard through the word of Christ" (Romans 10:17). God now delivers his message to us through his written Word.

In a sense we Christians now serve as God's Pony
Express. It is to us and not the angels that Jesus gave the
command to "go into all the world and preach the good
news to all creation" (Mark 16:15). It is to us and not the
angels that Jesus said, "You will be my witnesses . . . to the
ends of the earth" (Acts 1:8). Instead of being out front
delivering the message, angels are now working behind the
scenes. They are sent by God to control the forces of evil so
that God's will may be done on earth as it is in heaven.

Protect from physical harm

As these first two chapters have pointed out, angels
wear several different hats. Sometimes they deliver messages as part of God's Pony Express. At other times they
keep law and order as part of God's rangers. It's easy to forget that angels are watching over us night and day. But
Scripture leaves no doubt that they are protecting us from
harm. Without their help we wouldn't stand a chance
against the enemy. Paul told the Ephesians, "Our struggle
is not against flesh and blood, but against the rulers,
against the authorities, against the powers of this dark
world and against the spiritual forces of evil in the heavenly realms" (6:12).

These words indicate that the enemy is powerful. But
God assures us we don't have to fight Satan and his gang
single-handedly. We have God's army of angels on our
side. They protect us from physical harm. Without the
protection of God's holy angels, the devil would devour us
in an instant. With the Lord's permission, Satan promptly
deprived Job of his health, wealth, and family. We would
suffer these same setbacks if God's angels didn't protect us
from physical harm. Psalm 34:7 tells us, "The angel of the
LORD encamps around those who fear him, and he delivers

them." Psalm 91:11,12 gives us this comforting promise: "He will command his angels concerning you to guard you in all your ways; they will lift you up in their hands, so that you will not strike your foot against a stone."

The Bible contains many examples of how angels protected God's people from physical harm. In a dream Jacob "saw a stairway resting on the earth, with its top reaching to heaven, and the angels of God were ascending and descending on it" (Genesis 28:12). This dream not only assured Jacob that God had heard his cry of repentance and had forgiven his sins; it also gave him the comfort that God and his angels would be with him and protect him.

The Lord gave Elisha and his servant this same promise of protection. During the night the army of Aram surrounded the city where they were staying. When they got up the next morning and saw the size of the enemy's army, the servant asked, "Oh, my lord, what shall we do?" (2 Kings 6:15). From a human viewpoint they didn't stand a chance. They were outnumbered. But Elisha knew they had an invisible army of angels fighting on their side. At his request the Lord also enabled his servant to see this powerful force. Verse 17 states, "The LORD opened the servant's eyes, and he looked and saw the hills full of horses and chariots of fire all around Elisha."

The prophet Daniel was also protected by angels. After spending a night in the lions' den, he told a surprised King Darius, "My God sent his angel, and he shut the mouths of the lions" (Daniel 6:22). Centuries later the Lord sent an angel to deliver Peter from prison (Acts 12).

Sometimes we concentrate on the troubles that plague us—the sudden accident, the serious illness, the unexpected expense. If we could only see all those problems that don't afflict us—the accident we avoid, the sickness we are spared, the car that doesn't break down, the furnace that doesn't need repair. God's angels are watching over us. They protect us from physical harm and may even spare us added expense.

At this point the question is often raised, "Does this mean each of us has a guardian angel?" God's Word doesn't answer that question specifically. Some support for this idea may be found in Matthew 18:10, where Jesus says: "See that you do not look down on one of these little ones. For I tell you that their angels in heaven always see the face of my Father in heaven." But whether God assigns each of us a guardian angel or whether we have a group of angels watching over us isn't clear in Scripture. The important thing is that God sends his angels to guard us from physical harm.

A common fear among children is darkness. Who of us doesn't remember pulling our covers over our heads as we lay in the darkness of the night? Or maybe we ran upstairs as fast as we could to escape the foreboding gloom of the basement. We were afraid that someone or something lurked in the darkness. Even though we outgrow these childish fears, they are often replaced by adult fears. As parents and grandparents we fear for our children's physical and spiritual welfare. As teenagers we are afraid about not being accepted by our peers. As husbands and wives we fear our marriage partner will die and leave us alone. As teachers and pastors we fear for those placed under our care. As doctors and medical staff we fear for our patients. But as Christians we don't have to be afraid. The same angels that protect us also watch over our loved ones. God's army of angels is there. And one of their orders is to protect us and our loved ones from physical harm.

Concerned about spiritual matters

Besides protecting God's people from physical harm, angels are also involved in the spiritual matters of God's church. They are concerned that God's people stay in the faith and that others are brought to faith. They are glad when the lost are found. Jesus states, "There is rejoicing in the presence of the angels of God over one sinner who repents" (Luke 15:10). Angels are also disturbed by problems in the church. Paul told women to dress appropriately when they gathered for public worship because to do otherwise would disturb the angels (1 Corinthians 11:10). When we sin, we not only grieve the Holy Spirit, but we also grieve the angels.

In the early church angels often played a key role in mission work. We have already mentioned how angels proclaimed the gospel message at Christmas, Easter, and the Ascension. Their role continued as the gospel spread. An angel guided Philip to the Ethiopian eunuch (Acts 8:26). Likewise, an angel told Cornelius, "Now send men to Joppa to bring back a man named Simon who is called Peter" (10:5). In each case the gospel scored another success.

As we carry out the Lord's work in our personal lives and through our worldwide mission efforts, we have the comfort that angels are helping us. As the Lutheran Confessions state, "The angels pray for us,"[1] and in Zechariah 1:12 we have an example of an angel praying for God's people.

Yet angels do more than "ask the Lord of the harvest . . . to send out workers into his harvest field" (Luke 10:2). Nor do they simply sit on the sidelines and cheer us on in our efforts. Angels also accompany us in our mission work. As we seek to conquer new frontiers with the gospel, the angels are the invisible horsemen who ride alongside us and support us every step of the way. They drive back Satan and his band of outlaws. They join in rounding up the sheep and bringing them safely into the Shepherd's fold. As the Lord sends us out to do his work, he gives us a double promise. He not only tells us that he will be with us but also assures us that the angels will be with us the whole way.

The mail must go through

It is often said that nothing can keep the mail from being delivered. "Neither rain, nor snow, nor sleet, nor hail can stop the mail," we are told. Angels show this same determination as they serve their Creator. No matter which hat angels are wearing, they are eager to carry out God's command. They do this willingly and gladly. In Psalm 103:20,21 David exclaims: "Praise the LORD, you his angels, you mighty ones who do his bidding, who obey his word. Praise the LORD, all his heavenly hosts, you his servants who do his will." This truth is reflected in the Third Petition of the Lord's Prayer: "Your will be done on earth as in heaven." On earth God's will is hindered by Satan and his evil army. But in heaven the angels carry out God's will without any interference from the devil.

Angels and the final frontier

When someone is close to death, we may speak about that person "hearing the angels sing." That statement is closer to the truth than we might imagine. For God not only sends his angels to watch over us while we live, but he also sends them to receive us when we die. Like spiritual pallbearers, the angels will usher our souls safely to the Savior's side.

In the story of the rich man and Lazarus, Jesus says that when the beggar died, "angels carried him to Abraham's side" (Luke 16:22). As we mentioned earlier, God's Pony Express also ushered the prophet Elijah to heaven (2 Kings 2:11). Like Enoch (Genesis 5:24), Elijah didn't even have to travel through "death valley" to get there.

The Bible also points out that angels will play a part in the final judgment. They will accompany Jesus when he comes with great glory in the clouds (Matthew 25:31). They will "come and separate the wicked from the righteous" (13:49) and "gather his elect from the four winds, from one end of the heavens to the other" (24:31). As God's rangers they will help make sure that justice is served once and for all.

The thought that we don't have to face the final frontier of life alone gives us great comfort. As the Good Shepherd, our Savior will lead us safely through that dark valley of death. Escorted by angels, he will make sure we arrive at our final destination safe and sound.

A day to remember angels

We may have never observed it. We may not even know it exists. But the church calendar has a special day to remember angels: St. Michael and All Angels Day. It falls on September 29. Perhaps it is time we gave more attention to these divine messengers who appear so often on the pages of Scripture.

Certainly our society is giving considerable attention to angels. In recent years numerous books have been written on the subject of angels. The religious section in a secular bookstore is sure to have not one but several volumes on the subject. In addition, specials about angels have been shown on TV, and people have told stories of how they were "touched by an angel."

This sudden interest in angels can be good. With all the crime, murder, violence, and other negative things that are on TV, it's good when we can focus on something as positive as angels. A word of caution is in place, however. Much of this new angel awareness deals with the subjective, personal encounters some have supposedly had with angels. While some of these experiences may be interesting and even real, they often overshadow the objective truths about angels presented in God's Word. As Christians we know angels are real not because some people were supposedly visited by an angel but because God reveals that they are real in Scripture.

Another thing we have to watch out for is that we don't replace God with the angels. We are not to trust the angels to protect us. We are to trust the God who created the angels and sends them to watch over his people.

Psalm 91 teaches us this truth. It presents us with the classic conflict of good versus evil. It pictures the enemy as a fowler that seeks to snare us with his trap and shoot us down with his deadly arrows. And it also gives us the comfort that angels will protect us from the "flaming arrows of the evil one" (Ephesians 6:16). The popular hymn "On Eagles' Wings" (*Christian Worship* [CW] 440) is based on this psalm and captures these thoughts in a beautiful way.

The main emphasis in Psalm 91, however, is not on the angels, but on the God who sends them. As the opening words state, "He who dwells in the shelter of the Most High will rest in the shadow of the Almighty. I will say of the LORD, 'He is my refuge and my fortress, my God, in whom I trust'" (verses 1,2). God deserves the credit for watching over us, not the angels. The angels are simply servants he sends to protect us from harm.

This is also the purpose of St. Michael and All Angels Day. It is not a day to worship the angels, but a day to remember angels and worship God. An angel revealed to the apostle John that only God is to be worshiped and not angels. In Revelation 14:6,7 the apostle relates, "Then I saw another angel flying in midair, and he had the eternal gospel to proclaim to those who live on the earth—to every nation, tribe, language and people. He said in a loud voice, 'Fear God and give him glory, because the hour of his judgment has come. Worship him who made the heavens, the earth, the sea and the springs of water.'" Later on the warning was even stronger. John states, "At this I fell at his feet to worship him. But [the angel] said to me, 'Do not do it! I am a fellow servant with you and with your brothers who hold to the testimony of Jesus. Worship God!'" (Revelation 19:10; see also 22:8,9).

Even though angels are worthy of our attention, they are not worthy of our worship. Even though they pray for us, they are not to be addressed in prayer. They are only creatures of God and fellow servants of the Savior. To worship, trust in, and pray to them rather than God is to practice idolatry. Instead, we are to join the angels in singing that hymn of praise: "Hallelujah! For our Lord God Almighty reigns. Let us rejoice and be glad and give him glory!" (Revelation 19:6,7).

3

The Angel of the Lord

Sheriff or Deputy?

The word *angel* is used over three hundred times in the Bible. Usually it refers to a created, spiritual messenger who serves God and cares for his people on earth. In some cases, however, it is evident that when the word *angel* is used, something more than a created being is meant. It's referring not to a messenger of God, but to God himself.

This is particularly true when the Bible uses phrases such as "the angel of the Lord" or "the angel of God." Therefore, when we encounter an angel of the Lord on the pages of Scripture, we cannot assume it is a created being. Rather, we have to determine the angel's identity and ask the question "Is this angel one of God's deputies or is he the Sheriff himself?"

The angel of the Lord as deputy

When the term *angel of the Lord* appears in the New Testament gospels or in the book of Acts, it always refers to a created angel. It was an angel of the Lord who appeared to Joseph in a dream (Matthew 1:20). Later an angel of the Lord directed Joseph to Egypt (2:13) and back to Israel (2:19). When Jesus was born, an angel of the Lord appeared to the shepherds (Luke 2:9). When Jesus rose from the dead, an angel of the Lord opened his tomb to show the world it was empty (Matthew 28:2). It was also an angel of the Lord who guided Philip to the Ethiopian eunuch (Acts 8:26) and freed Peter from prison (12:7). On a more negative note, it was an angel of the Lord who struck down King Herod (12:23). Each time, God sent one of his angel deputies to carry out his will.

The angel of the Lord as sheriff

It is in the Old Testament or in the book of Revelation in the New Testament where the term *angel* or *angel of the Lord* often refers to something more than a created angel. To determine whether we are dealing with a deputy or with the Sheriff of heaven and earth, we have to look at the context. Just as lawmen often wear a badge to show their credentials, so there are times when the angel of the Lord reveals that he is not only sent by God, but is God.

Sometimes there is not enough evidence to make a positive identification. For example, we don't know if the angel who delivered Hezekiah from Sennacherib, king of Assyria, was the Sheriff or one of his deputies. 2 Kings 19:35 states, "That night the angel of the LORD went out and put to death a hundred and eighty-five thousand men in the Assyrian camp." From this account we can't determine the identity of this angel. The parallel account in 2 Chronicles 32:21 is even less specific when it says that "the LORD sent an angel" to carry out this task. On the basis of the evidence, we can't say if it was a created angel or God himself appearing as the angel of the Lord.

Many times in the Old Testament, however, we can make a positive identification. The first time the angel of the Lord appears in Scripture is to Hagar, the handmaid of Abram's wife, Sarai. When Sarai mistreated her, Hagar fled into the desert. Genesis 16:7 tells us, "The angel of the LORD found Hagar." Later, this angel promised, "I will so increase your descendants that they will be too numerous to count" (verse 10). Even Hagar knew it was more than a created angel who gave this promise. Verse 13 tells us, "She gave this name to the LORD who spoke to her: 'You are the God who sees me,' for she said, 'I have now seen the One who sees me.'"

This same angel of the Lord appeared to her again at a later date. At the Lord's direction Abraham sent Hagar and her son away. When they were at the point of desperation, Genesis 21:17 states, "The angel of God called to Hagar from heaven." Once again this angel promised to make her son into a great nation—a promise only God could give.

The angel of the Lord also appeared to Abraham when he was on Mount Moriah with his son Isaac. As he was about to sacrifice Isaac, the Bible tells us, "The angel of the LORD called out to him from heaven, . . . 'Do not lay a hand on the boy. . . . Do not do anything to him. Now I know that you fear God, because you have not withheld from me your son, your only son'" (Genesis 22:11,12).

Only God could make such a statement. It wasn't a deputy but the Sheriff—God himself—who appeared to Abraham on Mount Moriah.

On many other occasions the angel of the Lord appeared to God's people. In some cases his identity is even clearer. When the angel of the Lord appeared to Jacob in a dream, he told him, "I am the God of Bethel" (Genesis 31:13). And when Moses was called to lead God's people out of Egypt, the account tells us, "The angel of the LORD appeared to him in flames of fire from within a bush" (Exodus 3:2). Later this angel identified himself as the "I AM" God, the gracious Lord who is from everlasting to everlasting and who shows mercy to his people.

One of the most awesome appearances of this angel was when he led the people of Israel out of Egypt. Exodus 14:19 tells us, "Then the angel of God, who had been traveling in front of Israel's army, withdrew and went behind them." In this case the angel's presence was visible in the pillar of cloud and the pillar of fire that guided and protected God's people. And when Moses was receiving the law on Mount Sinai, the Lord told him: "See, I am sending an angel ahead of you to guard you along the way and to bring you to the place I have prepared. Pay attention to him and listen to what he says. Do not rebel against him; he will not forgive your rebellion, since my Name is in him" (Exodus 23:20,21). This angel of the Lord not only led the people of Israel out of Egypt but brought them into the Promised Land of Canaan.

Besides those we have mentioned, the angel of the Lord also appeared to Joshua (Joshua 5), Gideon (Judges 6), and Samson's parents (Judges 13). In each case, the Bible reveals that this angel was God himself. It is striking that the angel of the Lord visited God's people especially during the period of the patriarchs and judges. This shows us that before the coming of the prophets, God used a special prophet, the angel of the Lord, to communicate with his people and comfort them with the promise of the Savior.

Looking at the book of Revelation, we once again see that context determines the identity of the angel. For example, the angel mentioned in Revelation 20:1 appears to be more than a created being. He is credited with seizing "the dragon, that ancient serpent, who is the devil" (verse 2) and throwing him into hell's prison. Since this refers to the redemptive work of our Savior, Jesus Christ, this angel would once again refer to the Son of God.

The angel of the Lord as the pre-incarnate Christ

In the Old Testament the angel of the Lord was often God himself. He spoke of himself as God and made promises only God could make. Yet on some occasions this angel also distinguished himself from God. Looking once again at Exodus 23:20,21, the Lord told Moses: "I am sending an angel ahead of you to guard you along the way and to bring you to the place I have prepared. Pay attention to him and listen to what he says. Do not rebel against him; he will not forgive your rebellion, since my Name is in him." Even though the Lord is sending this angel, the one he is sending is to be obeyed and respected as God.

This same distinction is apparent when the Lord appeared to Abraham on Mount Moriah. The angel of the Lord told him, "Now I know that you fear God, because you have not withheld from me your son, your only son" (Genesis 22:12). Here again the angel not only spoke about God, but referred to himself as God.

These sections may seem puzzling until we remember the mystery of the Trinity—three persons in one God. All three are one God, yet all three are distinct persons.

Since the Father does the sending, this angel of the Lord would have to be either the Son or the Holy Spirit. It is unlikely that this angel would refer to the Holy Spirit since many Old Testament passages refer specifically to that member of the Trinity. This would lead us to conclude that this angel of the Lord is the Son of God before he became true man as the child of Mary.

Even though we celebrate Jesus' birth in Bethlehem, he also existed in Old Testament times, not as the God-man, but as true God. Like the other members of the Trinity, Jesus is also true God from all eternity. He was there when God the Father "spoke, and it came to be" (Psalm 33:9) and when "the Spirit of God was hovering over the waters" (Genesis 1:2). Jesus stressed his eternal nature when he told some unbelieving Pharisees, "Before Abraham was born, I am!" (John 8:58).

But how can we be sure that this angel of the Lord was really the pre-incarnate Christ? More convincing proof is found in the many New Testament passages that point out that Jesus was sent by the Father to proclaim God's Word. The night before his death Jesus told his disciples, "These words you hear are not my own; they belong to the Father who sent me" (John 14:24). And after his resurrection Jesus once again told his followers, "As the Father has sent me, I am sending you" (John 20:21). This would lead us to conclude that the angel of the Lord whom God sent in Old Testament times was often the pre-incarnate Christ.

Just as the Father sent his Son to proclaim the message of life in the New Testament, so he often sent him as his special messenger in Old Testament times. As John tells us, "The Word became flesh and made his dwelling among us" (John 1:14). This "Word" revealed God's will to people in the Old Testament era as well as in the New Testament times. He was God's special prophet sent to proclaim God's message to the world. Through his Word this angel of the Lord continues to reveal his will to us today, that all who call upon the name of the Lord will be saved.

4

The Fall of the Evil Angels

Good Gone Bad

John Wesley Hardin should have turned out right. His father was a Texas preacher and circuit rider who named his son after a man he greatly admired, the famed Methodist leader John Wesley. As a man of the cloth, he gave his son the best training he could.

In spite of his good upbringing, John Wesley Hardin was a classic case of good gone bad. He shot his first man—an ex-slave—at age 15. In the next two years he killed six more times. In an effort to run from the law, Hardin joined a cattle drive, where his killing continued. He killed six people on the drive and three more at the trail's end.

Hardin always maintained that he never killed someone who didn't need killing. Yet the truth is, wherever he went he always found someone he felt needed to be killed. By his late 20s he was wanted in connection with the death of some 30 people. All this earned him the title "the bloodiest gunman in Texas."

Hardin's case is nothing compared to the evil angels. They had more than a good upbringing—they were created perfect. They weren't just raised in a parsonage; their original home was heaven. But instead of choosing to stay on the straight and narrow, they turned to a life of crime. These angels started out good, but ended up being a case of good gone bad.

Time of their fall

The Bible doesn't tell us when Satan and his gang of outlaws were organized. Yet it does put it within a certain time frame.

Some Bible interpreters place it at the beginning of time. They feel that the opening words of Genesis reflect Satan's fall. They believe this is the reason why "the earth was formless and empty" and why "darkness was over the surface of the deep" (Genesis 1:2). According to this view, God carried out the creation process to restore order to the world.

This idea doesn't line up with the rest of God's Word, however. When creation was completed on the sixth day, we are told, "God saw all that he had made, and it was very good" (Genesis 1:31). Since angels are created beings, God would not have made this statement if some of the angels had already sinned. All God's creation—including the angels—was perfect.

Scripture indicates that Satan must have sinned after the creation of the world. Yet it also must have happened before the fall of man, since Satan tempted Adam and Eve to sin.

But how much time passed from the creation of Adam and Eve to their subsequent fall? Although the Bible is also silent about this, it appears to have been a rather short period of time. This is supported by the fact that Adam and Eve had no children prior to the fall. As perfect and holy people, they would have been eager and willing to carry out God's commands, including the one to "be fruitful and increase in number" (Genesis 1:28). Since they possessed both the desire and the ability to have children, their childlessness seems to indicate that days rather than years separated their creation from their fall. On one of these days Satan became the first tragic case in God's creation of good gone bad.

Nature of their crime

Scripture indicates that some angels rebelled against God. Second Peter 2:4 points out that "God did not spare angels when they sinned." Exactly what their sin was we are not told. Since "pride goes before destruction" (Proverbs 16:18), some suggest pride as the original crime. In 1 Timothy 3:6 there may also be a hint that pride was the original sin of the devil. Paul says that an overseer should not be a recent convert, "or he may become conceited and fall under the same judgment as the devil."

Ezekiel 28 would support this view. Even though these words were addressed to the wicked king of Tyre, it appears that the Lord was comparing him to Satan. If so, the account gives us some details about the devil's creation, fall, and eventual destruction. The holy writer states:

You were the model of perfection,
    full of wisdom and perfect in beauty.
You were in Eden,
    the garden of God;
    every precious stone adorned you:
    ruby, topaz and emerald,
    chrysolite, onyx and jasper,
    sapphire, turquoise and beryl.
Your settings and mountings were made of gold;
    on the day you were created they were prepared.
You were anointed as a guardian cherub,
    for so I ordained you.
You were on the holy mount of God;
    you walked among the fiery stones.
You were blameless in your ways
    from the day you were created
    till wickedness was found in you.
Through your widespread trade
    you were filled with violence,
    and you sinned.
So I drove you in disgrace from the mount of God,
    and I expelled you, O guardian cherub,
    from among the fiery stones.
Your heart became proud
    on account of your beauty,
and you corrupted your wisdom
    because of your splendor.
So I threw you to the earth;
    I made a spectacle of you before kings.
By your many sins and dishonest trade
    you have desecrated your sanctuaries.
So I made a fire come out from you,
    and it consumed you,
and I reduced you to ashes on the ground
    in the sight of all who were watching.
All the nations who knew you
    are appalled at you;

you have come to a horrible end
and will be no more (Ezekiel 28:12-19).

Another section that may refer to Satan is Isaiah 14:12-15. The prophet states:

How you have fallen from heaven,
O morning star, son of the dawn!
You have been cast down to the earth,
you who once laid low the nations!
You said in your heart,
"I will ascend to heaven;
I will raise my throne
above the stars of God;
I will sit enthroned on the mount of assembly,
on the utmost heights of the sacred mountain.
I will ascend above the tops of the clouds;
I will make myself like the Most High."
But you are brought down to the grave,
to the depths of the pit.

Once again the immediate context points to an earthly ruler, the king of Babylon. Recognizing that prophecy sometimes can speak about two similar people or events in one passage, it is possible that the fall of the king in this prophecy could be speaking about both the king of Babylon and Satan. This section explains how the name Lucifer came to be used for Satan. The Latin translation of the Hebrew Old Testament used the word "Lucifer" in Isaiah 14:12, as did the King James Version. The word "Lucifer" means "morning star," which is how the NIV translates the word. The title could refer to the special place Satan held among the stars of heaven—the angels. Note that in Revelation 22:16 Morning Star is a name for Christ.

Whatever specific crime Satan committed, it was contrary to God's holy will. It was aimed at removing God from his throne and placing himself as the ruler of the

earth. Satan may have tipped his hand when he promised
Adam and Eve, "You will be like God, knowing good and
evil" (Genesis 3:5). Satan knew from personal experience
how false this statement was. He had deceived himself
with this same lie.

Armed and dangerous

It's comforting to know that the good angels are numerous. But what about those that sinned? How many joined
Satan's rebellious band of outlaw angels? God's Word
reveals that more than a handful of angels fell into sin.
When Jesus healed the Gerasene man who was demon-
possessed, the demon told him, "My name is Legion . . .
for we are many" (Mark 5:9).

During a vision, the apostle John witnessed what may
be the fall of the evil angels. Revelation 12:3,4 tells us:
"Then another sign appeared in heaven: an enormous red
dragon with seven heads and ten horns and seven crowns
on his heads. His tail swept a third of the stars out of the
sky and flung them to the earth." Remembering that
angels are often called stars, this passage reveals that a
third of the angels followed Satan in his rebellion. Since
the book of Revelation contains many symbolical numbers, it would be hard to say that exactly one third of the
angels fell. Yet it does indicate the number was significant.

Perhaps it would be good to distinguish between the
terms *devil* and *demon*. Even though they are often used
interchangeably, we might speak of *one* devil but *many*
demons. The Bible reveals that Satan, or the devil, is the
chief of the evil angels. Matthew 25:41 reveals that hell
itself was created not as a place of punishment for human
beings, but was "prepared for the devil and his angels."
Satan has a sizable gang of outlaws who joined him in his

rebellion. While they vary in power, they all stand against everything good.

Like the good angels, Satan and his gang are powerful spiritual beings. They possess powers superior to our human abilities. Scripture reveals that they are able to do "all kinds of counterfeit miracles, signs and wonders, and . . . every sort of evil that deceives those who are perishing" (2 Thessalonians 2:9,10). Jesus warns that toward the end of time "false Christs and false prophets will appear and perform great signs and miracles" (Matthew 24:24). These counterfeit miracles will be so impressive they would "deceive even the elect—if that were possible" (verse 24).

Pharaoh's magicians are an example of how the devil can do counterfeit miracles. When the Lord sent Moses to deliver his people out of Egypt, he gave him the power to do miracles. At first Pharaoh's magicians were able to duplicate these signs through their secret arts. But even then an amazing thing happened. The Bible tells us: "Moses and Aaron went to Pharaoh and did just as the LORD commanded. Aaron threw his staff down in front of Pharaoh and his officials, and it became a snake. Pharaoh then summoned wise men and sorcerers, and the Egyptian magicians also did the same things by their secret arts: Each one threw down his staff and it became a snake. But Aaron's staff swallowed up their staffs" (Exodus 7:10-12).

Satan's office contains a copy machine that can duplicate some miracles of God. Yet its features are limited. It produces only a cheap replica of the real thing. As Christians we need to remember that our faith isn't based on signs and wonders which may look impressive at the time. "A wicked and adulterous generation looks for a miraculous sign" (Matthew 16:4). Our faith is based on the living Word, which proclaims a living Lord. The "sign of the prophet Jonah" (Matthew 12:39)—namely, Jesus' death, burial, and resurrection (verses 40,41)—is proof that we will live with God in heaven.

Another power that demons possess is the ability to invade our minds and influence our thoughts. When Peter confronted Ananias with his sin of deceit, he asked him, "How is it that Satan has so filled your heart that you have lied to the Holy Spirit . . . ?" (Acts 5:3). In 2 Corinthians 4:4 the apostle Paul says that the devil "has blinded the minds of unbelievers, so that they cannot see the light of the gospel." He also calls Satan "the spirit who is now at work in those who are disobedient" (Ephesians 2:2). Satan's ability to read our minds is also evident with those who deal with demon possession. The demon may respond to what a person thinks. Or the person who is possessed may actually carry on a conversation with the demon through thoughts rather than words. This would be different from a schizophrenic, who may hear voices. In the case of a possessed person, there may be an actual conversation that takes place in the mind between the possessed and the possessor.

But while the devil may know a lot about us and our thoughts, he is not all-knowing. Nor is he all-present, as God is. As a spiritual being, Satan is confined to a specific place at a certain time. But through his many demons he can be "present" in many places at the same time, exerting a strong influence on our lives and tempting us to sin.

Satan's power is inferior to God's, yet it is superior to our human abilities. For this reason Paul warns us: "Put on the full armor of God so that you can take your stand against the devil's schemes. For our struggle is not against flesh and blood, but against the rulers, against the authorities, against the powers of this dark world and against the spiritual forces of evil in the heavenly realms" (Ephesians 6:11,12). Adam and Eve's first encounter with the devil also indicates Satan's superior skills. He knew exactly what to say to Eve in order to lead her to doubt God's goodness (Genesis 3:1-7). Paul warns that Satan has the ability to outwit us (2 Corinthians 2:11). He can even appear as an angel of light (11:14).

We can learn something about the devil's intelligence and power from the temptation of Jesus. We might compare it to a card game in a Western saloon. In the first hand Satan challenged Jesus by playing some pretty good cards. He said to Christ, "If you are the Son of God, tell this stone to become bread" (Luke 4:3). The devil was laying a trap for Jesus. He wanted Jesus to believe that if he played his cards right, he could kill two birds with one stone. Jesus had been fasting and was hungry. By changing stones into bread, he could not only provide himself some food; he could also prove he was the famous lawman he claimed to be: the Son of God and the Sheriff of heaven and earth. But Jesus wasn't fooled by this little trick. He told Satan, "It is written: 'Man does not live on bread alone'" (verse 4).

In the second hand the devil dealt Jesus another real temptation. Luke tells us: "The devil led him up to a high place and showed him in an instant all the kingdoms of the world. And he said to him, 'I will give you all their authority and splendor, for it has been given to me, and I can give it to anyone I want to. So if you worship me, it will all be yours'" (verses 5-7).

This temptation shows that the devil has supernatural power. He showed Jesus in an instant all the kingdoms of the world. This is something only a creature of exceptional strength and ability could accomplish.

This temptation also shows Satan's wisdom. It hits at the heart of Jesus' redemptive work. The devil knew Jesus came to win back the world. Both Christ and the devil knew the painful path that lay ahead. Here the devil was offering Jesus an easy way out. He was telling him: "You don't have to go to Calvary. You don't have to endure all that pain and suffering. If you want the world back, here it is. Worship me and it will all be yours!" Once again Jesus responded with a card from the deck of Scripture. He answered, "It is written: 'Worship the Lord your God and serve him only'" (verse 8).

Yet the card game wasn't over. Satan had an ace up his sleeve. Jesus had won the first two rounds by playing a card from God's Word. So the devil tried the same approach. He took Jesus to the top of the temple and told him to jump off. And he quickly added, "He will command his angels concerning you to guard you carefully; they will lift you up in their hands, so that you will not strike your foot against a stone" (verses 10,11). But Jesus didn't fall for this little card trick of the devil either. To do so would be tempting God and not trusting him. Relying on God's clear and certain Word, Jesus could see through these strategies of Satan and played a perfect round, sending the devil away defeated.

But even though the devil displayed his supernatural skills in the temptation of Jesus, there are other times when he revealed his ignorance and stupidity. This was evident in the passion of Christ. Certainly the devil knew the prophecies concerning Jesus' life and death. Back in Eden the Lord had told him that the Savior would crush his head. An intelligent Satan would have tried to prevent Jesus from going to the cross, and there were times when the devil did. Jesus was hitting the nail on the head when he told Peter, "Get behind me, Satan!" (Matthew 16:23). Peter was trying to dissuade Jesus from going to the cross, the very thing an intelligent Satan would try to do.

The devil was digging his own grave, however, when he entered the heart of Judas. He was shooting himself in the foot when he led the Jewish leaders to arrest Jesus. And he was slipping the noose around his own neck when he incited the crowd to call out, "Crucify him! Crucify him!" By doing so he helped Jesus win a decisive victory.

It is interesting that those who deal with demon possession encounter this same thing in evil spirits. In his book *Hostage to the Devil*, Malachi Martin states:

> Every exorcist learns that he is dealing with some force or power that is at times intensely cunning, sometimes supremely intelligent, and at other times capable of crass stupidity; and it is both highly dangerous and terribly vulnerable.
>
> Oddly, while this spirit or power or force knows some of the most secret and intimate details of the lives of everyone in the room, at the same time it also displays gaps in knowledge of things that may be happening at any given moment of the present.[2]

The evil angels are powerful and knowledgeable. Yet their power and knowledge are limited. The more we study God's Word, the more we will possess a wisdom superior to that of Satan and his gang. And the more we will be able to recognize their evil ways.

Ranks among the evil angels

Just as there are ranks among the good angels, so it seems there may also be ranks of power in Satan's gang. If we understand Ezekiel 28 as a reference also to Satan, that would have put him into a prestigious category of angels—the cherubs. These are the angels that surround the throne of God and serve as his honor guard. The Jews in Jesus' day spoke of Satan as "the prince of demons" (Matthew 9:34; 12:24). And Jesus spoke of the eternal punishment of hell as being "prepared for the devil and his angels" (25:41), clearly ranking Satan as the leader of the other evil angels.

There may also be degrees of wickedness within Satan's gang. Jesus explains: "When an evil spirit comes out of a man, it goes through arid places seeking rest and does not find it. Then it says, 'I will return to the house I left.' When it arrives, it finds the house swept clean and put in order. Then it goes and takes seven other spirits more wicked than itself, and they go in and live there. And the final condition of that man is worse than the first" (Luke 11:24-26).

Many outlaws were given colorful nicknames. These names said something about who they were and what they did. We think of people like Billy the Kid—who had a scrawny, boyish appearance—and Lame Johnny—a horse thief with a noticeable limp. Scripture also gives quite a few names to the outlaw Satan. These names tell us something about his power and position. *Satan* means "enemy" and labels him an outlaw. His other most common name, devil, means "liar" or "slanderer." He is even called the father of lies since he deceived Adam and Eve with a lie and has been a compulsive liar ever since. No matter how smooth-talking this outlaw may be, we are to remember he speaks nothing but lies. Jesus said that lying is Satan's native language (John 8:44).

Besides these two names, Satan is also called Abaddon and Apollyon (Revelation 9:11), which mean "the destroyer"; Beelzebub (Luke 11:15), which means "lord of the flies"; and Belial (2 Corinthians 6:15), which means "worthlessness." The devil is also referred to as a murderer (John 8:44), a red dragon (Revelation 12:3), the ancient serpent (Revelation 20:2), the prince of this world (John 12:31), the ruler of the kingdom of the air (Ephesians 2:2), the spirit who is now at work in those who are disobedient (Ephesians 2:2), the evil one (Ephesians 6:16), the tempter (1 Thessalonians 3:5), a roaring lion (1 Peter 5:8), and the god of this age (2 Corinthians 4:4). All these expressions warn us that Satan is a dangerous outlaw that we are to avoid.

Bad blood

Like any ringleader, the devil has much "bad blood." Just as outlaws often made a life out of robbing banks and holding up trains and stagecoaches, so it is with Satan's gang. But instead of stealing money, Satan and his gang steal souls. They rob people of hope in life and confidence in death. They snatch away the seed of the gospel before it can grow in people's hearts.

Satan does this in a number of ways. Usually we think of the devil as the tempter. This was his original role in Eden, and he has played it well ever since. His temptations come in many different forms. Sometimes he tries to catch us in a sin. Greed, selfishness, and sexual immorality are some common traps set by the devil. He bates us with the promise of instant pleasure. Yet the joyride is short and comes at a high cost.

At other times the devil may tempt us by afflicting us with evil. Job is a good example. Satan caused Job to lose all his children and possessions in a single day. He was confident this man of God would curse God to his face

(Job 1:11). In this way the devil tries to get us to give up on God. He gets us to think that a loving God would never let something bad happen to one of his children. Yet God doesn't send his angels to protect us from all harm. Sometimes he allows misfortune to afflict us. But as we see in the life of Job, the Lord uses even the devil's devious ways for our good.

Besides being the tempter, Satan is also "the accuser of our brothers, who accuses them before our God day and night" (Revelation 12:10). This accuser role is also an effective way to steal souls.

The devil played both roles in robbing Judas of his salvation. First he came as the tempter. He knew Judas had a weakness for money. As treasurer for the disciples, Satan led Judas to "help himself to what was put into [the money bag]" (John 12:6). Satan incited him to object when Mary anointed Jesus' feet with expensive perfume. Judas claimed to care about the poor, but as one of Satan's gang, he cared only about himself. This greed eventually caused him to sell his Savior for a meager sum—30 silver coins. In all this Satan served as the tempter.

Yet when Jesus was sentenced to die, Judas changed his mind. The situation wasn't turning out as expected. The money he formerly loved now gave him no pleasure. In desperation he brought it back to the chief priests and confessed, "I have sinned . . . for I have betrayed innocent blood" (Matthew 27:4). Then Satan put on a different hat. Instead of tempting Judas to sin, Satan accused him of his sin. Satan made Judas feel his sin was so great that not even the Savior he betrayed could help him. This led Judas to despair and commit suicide. The tempter and accuser had gunned down another victim.

We also need to recognize these two hats Satan wears. If he can't tempt us to sin, he may accuse us of sin and try to convince us that there can be no forgiveness for us in Christ or in any other way. When faced with the guilt of our sin, we have to ask ourselves, "Who is doing the accusing?" Is God's law revealing our self-righteous attitude and showing us our need to repent? Or is the devil attacking our faith in Christ and leading us to despair of being saved? One leads us to feel the need for a Savior and say: "What a wretched man I am! Who will rescue me from this body of death?" (Romans 7:24). The other leads us to conclude that there is no Savior and leaves us in hopelessness and despair.

When the devil tries to accuse us of sin, we can respond with the words of Paul: "Who will bring any charge against those whom God has chosen? It is God who justifies. For I am convinced that neither death nor life, neither angels nor demons, neither the present nor the future, nor any powers, neither height nor depth, nor anything else in all creation, will be able to separate us from the love of God that is in Christ Jesus our Lord" (Romans 8:33,38,39). Christ has not only freed us from the accusations of Satan; he has also freed us from the accusations of God's law as well. Because Christ lived a perfect life in our place, we can now stand blameless before the throne of God.

5

A Look at the Occult

Gambling with the Devil

Many of the outlaws in the Wild West were gamblers. Since every game had its loser, tempers would often flare and fights would follow, sometimes leading to death. The legendary Wild Bill Hickok was one casualty. He was playing poker in Deadwood, South Dakota, when Jack McCall, whom he had beaten at cards, entered the saloon and shot him in the back.

Gambling with the devil can also be a deadly game. This will become clear as we take a journey into the occult and see some of the games people play with the devil. While these games may seem innocent at first, they are often the first step toward a deadly encounter with the devil.

The gamble of divination

One of the oldest games of the devil is divination. This is the art of using the devil's help to obtain information about secret things we could otherwise not know.

The Bible teaches that predicting the future is possible. At certain times the Lord gave his prophets the ability to foresee future events. Joseph was able to predict seven years of plenty and seven years of famine when he interpreted Pharaoh's dreams (Genesis 41). The prophet Daniel saw the various kingdoms that would come to power in the future, climaxing with the Roman Empire (Daniel 7).

Sometimes the Lord also enabled his prophets to know what was happening in a different location in the present. Samuel assured Saul that the donkeys he lost were found (1 Samuel 9:20). This is something Samuel would not have known without the Lord's help.

Some of the clearest prophecies in the Bible deal with the coming of Christ. Isaiah predicted the Messiah would be born of a virgin (7:14) and would be led like a lamb to the slaughter (53:7). Micah predicted the Savior would be born in Bethlehem (5:2). Zechariah foretold the events of Palm Sunday (9:9). David predicted Jesus would be despised by men and forsaken by God (Psalm 22). And prophecy is by no means confined to the Old Testament. In Revelation John sees the final days of this earth and the future glory of heaven.

The difference between biblical prophecy and divination, however, is as great as the difference between heaven and hell. The former is a revelation from God; the latter, a tool of the devil.

Trusting the devil to give us accurate information about the future is foolish for several reasons. For one thing, the devil's knowledge is limited. As a fallen angel his abilities are superior to ours. He may know things that are hidden to us. On the basis of this knowledge he can make some educated guesses about the future. Yet the devil is not all-knowing. Nor does he know what the future will hold. In Isaiah 41:22,23 the Lord states: "Bring in your idols to tell us what is going to happen. Tell us what the former things were, so that we may consider them and know their final outcome. Or declare to us the things to come, tell us what the future holds, so we may know that you are gods." This is a challenge that neither Satan nor his idols can meet. When asked about the future, the devil comes up empty. But even if he does know some things we don't, we can hardly trust this "father of lies" to tell us the truth. He will manipulate whatever he does know for his evil purposes.

The devil does not know future events. Nor can he control them. He is still subject to the almighty God, who guides the course of history for his purposes. And the Lord will use the devil's evil designs to further his own good plans. Nevertheless, many still look to Satan for insights on future events.

The art of divination can be traced back to Eden. The devil predicted a bright future for Adam and Eve once they ate of the forbidden fruit. Just the opposite came true. The result of that first prediction tells us something about the devil and his art of divination—neither can be trusted.

Throughout the centuries, divination was regularly practiced among the heathen nations of the world, sometimes even in sinful weakness by God's people. Laban told his nephew Jacob, "I have learned by divination that the LORD has blessed me because of you" (Genesis 30:27).

Divination is listed among the sins for which the Lord punished the northern tribes of Israel: "They practiced divination and sorcery and sold themselves to do evil in the eyes of the LORD, provoking him to anger" (2 Kings 17:17).

The cards in the devil's deck of divination are diverse. The book of Ezekiel mentions some methods used by the king of Babylon: "The king of Babylon will stop at the fork in the road, at the junction of the two roads, to seek an omen: He will cast lots with arrows, he will consult his idols, he will examine the liver" (21:21). The practice of analyzing the entrails of animals was also common among the ancient Greeks and Romans.

A wide variety of methods is also used in divination today. Methods range from card laying to palm reading to crystal gazing.

As a form of the occult, divination is condemned in Scripture. The Lord told his Old Testament people, "Let no one be found among you . . . who practices divination" (Deuteronomy 18:10). The prophet Samuel stressed the seriousness of this sin when he rebuked a disobedient Saul. Samuel warned him, "Rebellion is like the sin of divination" (1 Samuel 15:23). Unfortunately this was a warning Saul didn't take to heart. Saul consulted the witch of Endor for the purpose of divination (1 Samuel 28).

Moses stated in a positive way the attitude God wanted his people to have: "The secret things belong to the LORD our God, but the things revealed belong to us and to our children forever, that we may follow all the words of this law" (Deuteronomy 29:29). Rather than consulting with the devil, the Lord commanded his people to trust him and his Word. He assured them that the Messiah would be coming soon. Through this Savior the Lord promised, "I will forgive their wickedness and will remember their sins no more" (Jeremiah 31:34).

Searching the stars

The most popular and visible form of divination today is astrology. Millions of Americans take tips from the horoscope columns that appear in 1,400 newspapers across the country. Many astrologers are proclaiming the Age of Aquarius, an era where so-called old-fashioned Christian values will give way to a new set of standards.

There is no doubt astrology has received renewed interest in recent years. Some of this may be due to the considerable credence it has received from politicians and celebrities. In England both Lady Diana and Sarah Ferguson, members of the royal family, have consulted with Penny Thornton, a prominent British astrologer whose column appears in Britain's *Today* newspaper.[3] In the late 1980s Americans were stunned to learn that Nancy Reagan regularly consulted with astrologer Joan Quigley. Before the president's schedule was arranged, the first lady would check the horoscope to see which dates were favorable. Many national and world events were planned according to the stars.

Astrologers believe that the position of the planets at one's birth determines one's personality, talents, and destiny. Some go so far as to call this belief a science. A recent poll indicates that 47 percent of Americans think astrology has some scientific truth.[4] Joan Quigley compares it to medical diagnosis. She insists that astrology "can tell you more about yourself than a psychiatrist can tell you after many hours of consultations on his couch."[5]

One doesn't have to dig too deeply into astrology to realize it is far from a science. Perhaps the point that

Signs of the Zodiac

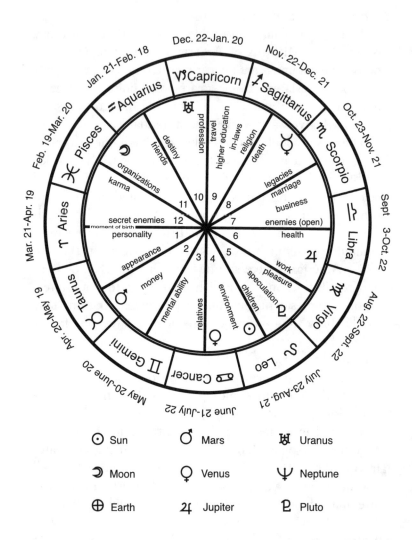

proves this the most is that the entire zodiacal calendar has changed in the past two thousand years. Because the sun arrives at the eastern horizon on March 21 a little earlier each year, it gradually moves from one astrological house to the other. This is called the precession of the equinoxes.[6] What this means is that about every 2,100 to 2,200 years the signs and dates of the zodiac change. Those whose birthdays fall between February 19 and March 20 presently call themselves Pisces. But actually they were born when the sun was in the sign of Aquarius. Likewise, those who call themselves Aquarians were actually born under the sign of Capricorn and so on.

A quick comparison of predictions will also show that astrology is far from an exact science. This is evident in the following predictions that three different astrologers made for 1994:

> "War by the end of the year, in Korea or Haiti."
> "We're in a fairly war-torn patch. Africa will be a blood-bath."
> "I don't see any really major war."[7]

Many personal horoscopes appear to be nothing more than conventional wisdom. Consider the following horoscope Jeane Dixon offered in her daily newspaper column: "Steer clear of people who make you tense. Taking careless chances could cost you money or someone's respect. Say 'no' to a dare. Ask someone else to drive if you have been drinking. Virtue triumphs!"[8] One has to wonder whether there is ever a time when this isn't good advice to follow. "Don't drink and drive" is good advice no matter how the stars are positioned. Likewise, it is seldom wise to take careless chances.

Besides offering practical advice, some horoscopes pretend to predict the future. But they are often so vague, one could find some form of fulfillment no matter what happens in the course of a day.

Where did this practice of astrology come from? It can be traced back to the ancient Babylonians. It was such a major part of their culture that their name was often associated with the practice. Since this form of divination posed a constant threat to his people, God clearly condemned it. Isaiah 47:13,14 states: "Let your astrologers come forward, those stargazers who make predictions month by month, let them save you from what is coming upon you. Surely they are like stubble; the fire will burn them up. They cannot even save themselves from the power of the flame."

As Christians we place our trust for the present and the future in the real Star of Bethlehem—Jesus Christ. He gave us this comforting prediction:

> There will be signs in the sun, moon and stars. On the earth, nations will be in anguish and perplexity at the roaring and tossing of the sea. Men will faint from terror, apprehensive of what is coming on the world, for the heavenly bodies will be shaken. At that time they will see the Son of Man coming in a cloud with power and great glory. When these things begin to take place, stand up and lift up your heads, because your redemption is drawing near (Luke 21:25-28).

It is a comfort knowing that our future is not in the hands of some astrologer but in the hands of an almighty God, who asked Job: "Can you bind the beautiful Pleiades? Can you loose the cords of Orion? Can you bring forth the constellations in their seasons or lead out the Bear with its cubs? Do you know the laws of the heavens? Can you set up God's dominion over the earth?" (Job 38:31-33). The key to our future isn't written in the stars. It is written on the cross and summed up in a few short words: "It is finished" (John 19:30). Our eternal future is certain and safe through the crucified Christ.

Playing games with the devil

One cannot help but notice an occult theme in certain popular games. An example is Dungeons & Dragons. Joan Hake Robie has spent considerable time studying the occult in its various forms. In her book *The Truth About Dungeons & Dragons*, she points out that besides promoting sex and violence, Dungeons & Dragons dabbles with spirits and promotes the occult. This is reflected in the bizarre list of characters used in the game, which includes demons, dragons, witches, zombies, gnomes, and creatures that cast spells and exercise supernatural powers.

Created by Gary Gygax in 1974, the game has retained its popularity over the years. Since Dungeons & Dragons is a complex game that requires a creative mind, it appeals to a certain group of people. Robie describes the typical player as a "white male teenager from a middle class background. He is above average in intelligence and interested in math and science. He is not particularly athletic and he reads a lot, especially science fiction and fantasy. He has a small circle of friends, mostly his own age, with whom he plays the game on a weekly or even daily basis."[9]

And what does this game involve? Dungeons & Dragons is a fantasy roleplaying game. The key person is the Dungeon Master, who creates a "dungeon." The goal of other players is to work their way through an elaborate maze filled with monsters and creatures in order to seize hidden treasure. To accomplish this, the players must resort to many different tactics, including murder, rape, and casting evil spells. Even though these actions are only imaginary, the players become acquainted with occult rituals and creatures.

Another danger is that players become deeply involved in the game and their particular creature. Some become so engrossed in the game that they spend every available moment playing out their part. This is not only a poor use of time, but it occupies the mind with occult characters and practices. As Christians we would do well to apply Paul's words in Philippians 4:8: "Finally, brothers, whatever is true, whatever is noble, whatever is right, whatever is pure, whatever is lovely, whatever is admirable— if anything is excellent or praiseworthy—think about such things."

Those who don't heed Paul's warning and instead devote themselves to devilish games such as Dungeons & Dragons may find themselves drawn deeper into the occult. One writer concludes, "Those who have come out of the occult tell us that D&D is one of the most comprehensive and effective training materials used to prepare young people for entrance into witchcraft."[10]

Another game that makes use of the occult is the Ouija board. The game was introduced to America in the late 1800s, but its roots go back many centuries. It was first marketed by the Baltimore Talking Board Company as a religious, and therefore nontaxable, item. Its popularity soared during the First World War, when people used it to contact friends and relatives who were overseas. When the Internal Revenue Service questioned the tax exempt status of the board in 1920, the company argued: "We contend that the Ouija Board is a form of amateur mediumship and not a game or sport. By means of this board one is enabled to get in touch with the other side."[11]

In 1966 Parker Brothers purchased the rights to the Ouija board and marketed it across the country. It can now be purchased at almost any department store.

The game is simple. It consists of a plastic message indicator and a board with the alphabet, the numbers 0 to 9, and the words "yes," "no," and "good bye" printed on the surface. In the directions provided on the box, players are told: "You and your partner sit at opposite sides of the board, with your fingers placed lightly on the message indicator. One of you asks a question. . . . Now concentrate very hard on the matter at hand—and wait for the indicator to move and begin to reveal the answer through its message window. Will it tell you YES . . . or NO? Will it give you a NUMBER . . . or SPELL out an answer?"

Although the game calls itself a "mystifying oracle," the impression is given that it is all in fun. However, it does leave the question open as to whether it is more than just a harmless game. On the back of the box it adds: "For decades, players have brought their questions to the OUIJA board. What you do with the information it reveals is between you—and the Mystifying Oracle! OUIJA . . . it's only a game—isn't it?" The board itself can answer this question. Those who have asked the oracle where it gets it power have received similar answers that point to the devil.

Studies have also shown that the Ouija board is another first step that may lead to more serious forms of occultism, including demon possession. Douglas Deen, the 14-year-old boy whose story was the basis for the movie *The Exorcist*, used a Ouija board regularly prior to being possessed.[12]

Satan sells

For the past several decades, occult themes have been common in the entertainment industry. Even though some see it only as an advertising gimmick, we cannot underestimate the power of the media. Whether we are talking about heavy metal music or the movie industry, it is clear that "Satan sells."

But are the people who introduce these occult themes really serious about the devil? In answer to that question we note that some heavy metal bands that use Satan to sell their products claim they don't take the occult seriously. In an industry where entertainers are constantly trying to outdo each other with bizarre and shocking acts, some see the occult as just another way to attract attention and make money.

Others are practicing Satanists. Jimmy Page, the lead guitarist for Led Zeppelin, became so fascinated with the occult he purchased the English castle once owned by the English Satanist and occultist Aleister Crowley. King Diamond was a member of Anton LaVey's Church of Satan. Black Sabbath concerts have even included black masses and invocations to the devil. Whether these people actually believe in the devil or are just using him as an advertising ploy, the result is the same. Songs are being sung to the glory of Satan.

To help us understand how deeply satanic some of the songs are, consider the following lyrics. The first are from a song by the heavy metal band AC/DC and entitled "Highway to Hell":

> Hey, Satan
> Paid my dues
> Hey, I'm in a rockin' band.
> Hey, Mama
> Look at me
> I'm on my way to the promised land.
> I'm on the highway to hell, highway to hell.

I'm on the highway to hell, highway to hell.
Don't stop me.[13]

In a song called "Sacrifice," the group Venom describes a sacrifice that is about to take place in a Black Mass:

Candles glowing, altars burn
Virgin's death is needed there
Sacrifice to Lucifer, my master
Bring the chalice, raise the knife
Welcome to my sacrifice
Plunge the dagger in her breast, I insist
S-A-C-R-I-F-I-C-E[14]

This is not to say that all rock groups are the tool of the devil. However, as Christians we need to use discretion in choosing music. Usually the CD cover or the song titles will reveal any occult leanings a group may have. Satanic symbols such as a goat's head, the number 666, an inverted pentagram, and a lightning bolt may be found there. Rather than outlawing all rock music in our homes, teaching our children to be selective with their music might be a better alternative. The argument "I just like the music and don't listen to the words" isn't true. Satanic rock is one more way the devil may package his lies in an attractive wrapper in order to sell them to an unsuspecting generation.

Besides rock music, the movie industry has also dabbled in occult themes. It started in the 1960s when the devil made his debut in *Rosemary's Baby*, a sacrilegious movie about a woman who supposedly conceived through the power of the devil. A few years later *The Exorcist* entered theaters. Once producers discovered that "Satan sells" on the silver screen, they flooded the market with occult movies such as *The Omen*, *Friday the 13th*, and others.

Being entertained by the devil is dangerous. But equally bad are the countless movies filled with foul language, sexual immorality and innuendo, a lack of respect for authority, violence, murder, and other vices. Being entertained by evil is just as dangerous as being entertained by the devil. In either case we can hear Satan inviting us, "Bow down and worship me." As Christians we need to repeat the prayer of Solomon: "Give your servant a discerning heart . . . to distinguish between right and wrong" (1 Kings 3:9).

In the hit single "The Gambler," singer Kenny Rogers makes this point: "You have to know when to hold them, know when to fold them, know when to walk away, know when to run." We need to show this same discretion when it comes to gambling with the devil. He has plenty of cards up his sleeve and is just waiting for the right time to play them. Instead of falling for his card tricks, let's call his bluff. As James 4:7 tells us, "Resist the devil, and he will flee from you." Satan bet everything he had on Calvary and lost. Because of what Christ did for us, we don't have to gamble on our salvation. We can be sure of it because of Christ.

6

Witchcraft and Other Forms of Spiritism

"Women of the Evening"

Prostitution was commonly practiced on the western frontier. "Women of the evening" often made their homes among outlaws, gamblers, and drinkers. In our journey through the occult, we now come to a spiritual house of prostitution. Here we find many different "women of the evening" practicing their craft. Even though we don't want to enter these places of ill repute, it is helpful to know what goes on inside them. For these are more of the forbidden arts Satan uses to seduce souls into following him.

The seduction of witchcraft

For many centuries, witchcraft was a hidden art. It was practiced in secret under the cover of darkness. But now, like many other sinful practices, it has started to come out of the closet. To overcome the common stereotype of witches found in fairy tales, witches today try to convince people they are like everyone else; they just follow a different form of religion.

Modern witches, a term that is applied to both men and women, call their practice "Wicca," "Wica," "Benevolent Witchcraft," or "The Craft." As a religion Wicca is recognized by the government and is protected by the First Amendment. Some claim that witchcraft is presently the fastest growing religion in the world. Whether this is based on fact or "witchful" thinking is difficult to say, since it is not a well-organized religion that keeps track of its membership.

Witches often refer to their craft as "The Old Religion." They do so in contrast to Christianity, which they consider a recent development. They claim that Wicca dates back thousands of years before Christianity and was the original religion of early man. Witches also blame Christianity for giving witchcraft a bad name. Ironically, Wiccans deny the existence of the devil, whom they call an invention of Christianity. They are also careful to distinguish themselves from Satanists.

What kind of religion is witchcraft? What are some of its beliefs? Witches are pantheistic in that "the Divine is seen as everywhere and in everything."[15] They are also animistic in that "every human, tree, animal, stream, rock, and other form of Nature [are] seen to have a Divine Spirit within."[16]

The Wiccan religion recognizes many gods, although two main deities are worshiped: the horned god of hunting and nature and the goddess of fertility. Of the two, the goddess usually receives more attention and is often worshiped as the earth mother. Even though there are many different traditions within witchcraft, they are united by a common thread—the worship of nature and the earth. One writer calls them the "spiritual aspect of the ecology movement."[17]

Selena Fox is the high priestess of Circle Sanctuary, a Wiccan group located in Mount Horeb, Wisconsin. Circle Sanctuary is headquartered on a two hundred-acre sacred nature preserve that features a variety of ritual sites and meditation places. Besides conducting regular rituals for witches, Circle Sanctuary also publishes a quarterly newsletter entitled *Circle Network News*. Fox explains that Wiccans "love and respect Nature and seek to live in harmony with the rest of the ecosphere. Many have personal communication and friendships with various animals, plants, and other lifeforms. They honor the cycles of Nature."[18]

Within the various traditions, witches gather in groups called "covens" or "circles," which include up to 13 people. Each coven is led by a high priest and a high priestess. Witch Raymond Buckland explains, "In many traditions, since the goddess, as a bearer of life, is perceived as being of somewhat greater importance than the god, so the priestess is regarded as slightly more important than the priest."[19] A high priestess may also start other covens, of which she becomes the witch queen. The emphasis given the goddess and the high priestess may explain why many feminists are attracted to The Craft. As one witch put it, "This goddess, who appealed to my feminist instincts, was a deity that I could respect."[20]

The coven serves as a type of support group for local witches. Covens meet regularly, especially at the time of the full moon. Witchcraft has four major *sabbats*, or festivals, including February Eve, May Eve, August Eve, and November Eve, which divide the year into four equal parts. In addition to these there are four lesser sabbats: the first day of spring, summer, fall, and winter. Fox adds that the October festival of Samhain, popularly known as Halloween, begins a new year in most Wiccan traditions.[21]

What happens during coven meetings? The coven will gather for rituals that include "a combination of meditation, invocations, movement, music, and the use of magical tools."[22] The high priestess will also read from the *Book of Shadows*, a personal diary containing Wiccan rituals and formulas. In some groups witches attend these meetings "skyclad," a Wiccan term meaning "naked." In other groups they wear loose robes. Those who are "clad only by the sky" claim that clothing prohibits the power of the earth from entering their bodies. While witches sometimes make use of charms and spells, they claim to practice only "white magick" in order to bring about positive change in the world and their personal lives. In the pledge that all witches must take to become members of Circle Sanctuary, this promise is made: "May I use the Force [psychic power] wisely and never use it for aggression nor for malevolent purposes."[23]

In spite of the positive picture witches present today, the religion is clearly pagan—a name Wiccans readily accept. Little do they realize that by accepting the title "pagan," they are also accepting the judgment of God that goes with it. The apostle Paul described them well when he wrote: "Although they claimed to be wise, they became fools and exchanged the glory of the immortal God for images made

The horned god of hunting and nature

to look like mortal man and birds and animals and reptiles. They exchanged the truth of God for a lie, and worshiped and served created things rather than the Creator—who is forever praised" (Romans 1:22,23,25). The apostle's words are especially fitting for witches when we remember the word *wicca* is an Old English word meaning "wise." The woman Witchcraft may appear to be wise and attractive on the outside. Yet as a spiritual woman of the evening she is out to seduce our souls.

The seduction of near-death experiences

Witchcraft and other forms of spiritism were regularly practiced in Old Testament times. Even though God clearly condemned these practices, he did at times use these evil arts for his purpose. One example is King Saul and the witch of Endor. When the Lord refused to answer unbelieving Saul, the king told his attendants, "Find me a woman who is a medium, so I may go and inquire of her" (1 Samuel 28:7). When they informed him that there was one in Endor, Saul consulted with her under the cover of night. The Bible records that through this woman, Saul was able to contact the spirit of Samuel.

Like unbelieving Saul, some also consult with mediums today in an effort to contact the dead. Somehow they feel that those who have died can provide them with information about the future.

A new form of spiritism that has risen up in recent decades surrounds near-death or out-of-body experiences. Due to advances in medical technology, people can sometimes be resuscitated and brought back "from the dead." Some describe encounters in which they supposedly left their bodies and experienced what lies beyond the grave. Many relate how they were drawn through a long tunnel with a bright light at the end. There they met a being of light whom they identify as God, Jesus, or an angel. They may also see departed friends or relatives. The entire scene gives them a feeling of peace, and while they want to stay, they are told that their time has not yet come and they have to return to their bodies. In many cases this experience gives them a new perspective on life and may alter their attitudes and lifestyles significantly.

But are these encounters real? Can a person actually experience heaven and come back to tell about it? The Bible reveals that getting a glimpse of heaven in this life is possible. In 2 Corinthians 12:2-4 Paul describes such an experience when he states: "I know a man in Christ who fourteen years ago was caught up to the third heaven. Whether it was in the body or out of the body I do not know—God knows. And I know that this man—whether in the body or apart from the body I do not know, but God knows—was caught up to paradise. He heard inexpressible things, things that man is not permitted to tell." The martyr Stephen also saw a picture of heaven as he was about to die (Acts 7:55,56). Likewise the book of Revelation was one big out-of-body experience for the apostle John.

But how should we as Christians react to these experiences? Should we assume all of them are real? On the basis of the Bible we cannot write off all near-death encounters as hoaxes. While a possible explanation may be a reaction to medications, a lack of oxygen to the brain, or the body responding to the shock of a traumatic situation, some encounters may be real. We do have to test near-death experiences, however, with God's Word, especially when we consider the popularity that other books on the subject currently enjoy in our society. Those who supposedly died but lived to tell about it are treated as gurus who proclaim a message of comfort, hope, and love. Their books are held up as proof that there is life after death.

A prominent figure in this area is Raymond Moody. Often called the father of the near-death experience, Moody has studied hundreds of cases of near-death experiences and written several books on the subject. Not only does Moody believe that such experiences are real, but he also sees them as a way to contact the dead. He has a special room filled with props designed to encourage contact with spirits and other occult phenomena. He claims that about half of those who use this room are able to make contact with deceased friends or relatives or even their personal guardian angel.

The Bible points out that near-death experiences are possible. Yet it also warns us about placing our trust in them. A good commentary on this subject is the story of the rich man and poor Lazarus (Luke 16:19-31). The rich man asked Abraham to send Lazarus back to his brothers. He argued, "If someone from the dead goes to them, they will repent" (verse 30). But Abraham replied, "If they do not listen to Moses and the Prophets, they will not be convinced even if someone rises from the dead" (verse 31).

The Bible gives us all the proof we need that there is life after death. It testifies to the resurrection of Christ. Therefore we will not only heed God's warning not to "consult the dead on behalf of the living" (Isaiah 8:19). We will also confess with Job: "I know that my Redeemer lives, and that in the end he will stand upon the earth. And after my skin has been destroyed, yet in my flesh I will see God; I myself will see him with my own eyes—I, and not another. How my heart yearns within me!" (19:25-27). Christ's resurrection proves that we too will rise from the dead.

The seduction of the New Age Movement

Imagine you are at a health seminar sponsored by the local hospital. In one of the sessions you are introduced to a woman who says she will help you deal with stress. In the course of her discussion, she asks you to close your eyes and picture a beautiful, peaceful scene. You are to imagine how you are at one with the world around you. This describes an incident the author had while attending a cardiology workshop for clergy offered by a hospital in the area. It gives us an idea how the Woman of the New Age seeks to seduce us into following her ways.

New Age thought can be found in almost every area of life: education, medicine, science, politics, psychology, entertainment, and religion. Its concepts can be found in training sessions at work and in movies our children watch at home. Proponents of the New Age include such diverse people as death-and-dying therapist Elizabeth Kübler-Ross, singer John Denver, and actress Shirley MacLaine, who is often called the high priestess of the New Age Movement. She has written a number of best-selling books on the subject, including *Out on a Limb*, which describes her conversion to the New Age philosophy.

Since the New Age is not an organized group or religion, defining its principles can be as difficult as nailing gelatin to a tree. *Time* magazine has called it "a cloudy sort of religion, claiming vague connections with both Christianity and the major faiths of the East . . . plus an occasional dab of pantheism and sorcery."[24] Others have termed it a "rag bag of ideas that display an amazing unity."[25]

In his book *Unmasking the New Age*, Douglas R. Groothuis offers the following six statements to summarize the New Age:[26]

1. ALL IS ONE—Groothuis explains: "Ultimately there is no difference between God, a person, a carrot, or a rock. They are all part of one continuous reality that has no boundaries, no ultimate division."[27]

2. ALL IS GOD—The New Age teaches that God is everything and everything is god. God is not regarded as a personal being, but an impersonal energy force. Everything that exists is god. This concept was evident in the *Star Wars* films with the presence of "the Force."

3. WE ARE ALL GOD—Since everything is god it follows that we are all gods. The key is to awaken the god within us. A noted New Age leader urges: "Kneel to your own self. Honor and worship your own being. God dwells within you as you!"[28]

4. A CHANGE OF CONSCIOUSNESS—Even though we are all gods, we don't know it. The problem is our ignorance, which keeps us from realizing our divinity. The solution is enlightenment. Through meditation we can alter our consciousness and open the door to reality.

5. ALL RELIGIONS ARE ONE—Religions are simply different paths to the one truth. Thus the New Age seeks to incorporate all religions into its movement. Christianity is no exception. Rather than being the Savior of the world, they say Christ's mission was to alert the sleeping masses to their innate divinity.

6. NEW AGE COMING—The old age is passing away. A new age is dawning. We are part of a great transformation of consciousness and culture. Through "conscious evolution" we will be able to steer the cosmic ship into bigger and better times. New Agers call this the Age of Aquarius. According to astrology, this will happen when the sun begins to rise in

Aquarius on the first day of spring. This will bring an end to the old age of Pisces, the fish, which some identify with the Christian era, since the fish was adopted as a symbol of Christianity. It will be replaced by the new age of Aquarius, which will include a new world order, universal peace, and a completely different set of values. But because the various boundaries of the zodiac are so poorly defined, astrologers do not agree on when this Age of Aquarius will begin.

From these six points we can see that the New Age Movement is more of a philosophy or worldview than it is an orderly set of beliefs. Yet its ties to the occult are clear. Besides books and magazines, a New Age bookstore will often contain an extensive list of items such as Tibetan bells, exotic herbal teas, Viking runes, solar energizers, colored candles, and other occult paraphernalia often used in New Age meditation.[29]

The most sacred object for many New Agers is crystal. They believe it provides a healthful energy field and possesses healing powers not present in other objects. Another claim is that it enhances meditation: "Add quartz crystals with your meditation and you will find that the meditative process is tremendously amplified and the results experienced more quickly."[30]

New Age thought has also fueled a sudden interest in angels. Many New Age psychics and channelers claim to have contact with an angel or spirit guide who gives them insights about life. Many others who say they have seen an angel describe the great peace they felt even though the Bible indicates that throughout history angel sightings were rare and those who experienced them were terrified.

What is missing most in the current angel craze is Christ. Many who testify to the existence of angels forget that angels testify to the existence of Christ. Angels' main task is to worship and serve the Lamb, not to provide people with mystical experiences or protect them from physical harm. To believe in angels without believing in Christ is to "follow deceiving spirits and things taught by demons" (1 Timothy 4:1). Angels protect us in this life and will finally carry us to the next life not because they are spiritual beings with supernatural powers. They will do this because it is the will of the Savior God they serve.

The more we study the New Age, the more we see it is nothing more than age-old lies of the devil. It echoes the promise Satan spoke in Eden when he told Eve, "You will be like God, knowing good and evil" (Genesis 3:5). Like the Woman of witchcraft and the Woman of the near-death encounter, the Woman of the New Age may look attractive on the outside. But as a spiritual woman of the evening, "her house is a highway to the grave, leading down to the chambers of death" (Proverbs 7:27). She is just one more way that Satan appears as an angel of light and tries to seduce the masses.

7

Demon Possession

Possessed by Evil

The lifestyle of an outlaw left much to be desired. Robbing banks, holding up trains, shooting, killing, drinking, gambling—these are only a few of the vices that characterized villains.

When we look at the trail of trouble they often left behind, we may wonder what possessed them to do such evil things. Certainly the devil was working hard in those days, just as he often works overtime today.

But while these outlaws were possessed by evil, other people have actually been possessed by a demon. Let's now enter the dark world of demon possession. And as we do, let's remember that our bodies are temples of the Holy Spirit. Through faith in Christ as our Savior, he possesses our hearts and lives. Christ bought us with his own blood, and we now belong to him, both body and soul. As Christians we stand firmly on the Rock the gates of hell cannot overcome—Jesus Christ.

The influence of the evil one

The devil and his gang of demons can possess some people. But he influences us all. Without actually entering our bodies and taking control, the devil can plant evil thoughts in our minds and confront us with temptations. Often much of the preparatory work has already been done by the unbelieving world or our own sinful nature. We have all sowed wild oats of our own.

But as an enemy of the church the devil sows weeds among the wheat at an alarming rate (Matthew 13:25,39). He snatches away the seed of the gospel before it can take root (verse 19). He enters our hearts and tries to steal away our souls as he did with Judas (Luke 22:3). Even without possessing our bodies, the devil poses a great threat to our physical and spiritual welfare.

One of Satan's greatest threats comes in the form of false teaching. The apostle Paul told Timothy: "The Spirit clearly says that in later times some will abandon the faith and follow deceiving spirits and things taught by demons. Such teachings come through hypocritical liars, whose consciences have been seared as with a hot iron" (1 Timothy 4:1,2).

Can't we see numerous examples of Satan's efforts? One of the most dangerous false teachings is the idea that there are no absolute rules of right and wrong. As a result, sin is sanitized and Christian values are attacked. Instead of taking a stand on important moral issues, people apply the principle "live and let live." Even churches accept sinners just as they are instead of calling them to repentance. All this is done in the name of love. Sometimes it is even done in the name of Christ.

As we live in a sinful society, we need to keep away from Satan's branding iron. Just as scar tissue is less sensitive to touch, so a seared conscience is less sensitive to sin. We would do well to heed the advice of 1 Peter 5:8,9: "Be self-controlled and alert. Your enemy the devil prowls around like a roaring lion looking for someone to devour. Resist him, standing firm in the faith, because you know that your brothers throughout the world are undergoing the same kind of sufferings."

Satan and his evil gang's influence through false doctrine is widespread. Their influence through bodily possession may be much more limited; nevertheless, it is just as real.

The demon-possessed in Bible times

Prior to the coming of Christ, we have only one possible case of demon possession reported in the Bible, that of King Saul. First Samuel 16:14 tells us, "The Spirit of the LORD had departed from Saul, and an evil spirit from the LORD tormented him." Just as the Lord allowed the devil to inflict evil on Job, so the Lord allowed an evil spirit to torment Saul. Whether this evil spirit actually took possession of Saul is not clear. Since this spirit often caused the king to have violent fits of rage, it would appear that we are dealing here with actual possession.

Another possible explanation for Saul's behavior is what some call obsession. Rather than actually possessing the person's body, a demon will harass and disturb the individual with paranormal activity. One writer explains:

"Such a person is constantly meeting unexplained obsta-
cles, having strange experiences in losing objects, or in
finding things in different places. Sometimes things will
shake or rattle in the room. Occasionally, too, the person's
sleep will be disturbed by mental or physical means, such
as shaking the bed or being awakened by a noise, such as a
picture falling off the wall."[31]

During the ministry of Christ, demon possession seemed
to reach epidemic proportions. It is almost as though the
devil unleashed his entire army, hoping to foil God's plan
of salvation.

Some suggest that those who are called demon-
possessed in the New Testament were simply suffering
from various diseases. They argue that Bible writers simply
reflected the conventional wisdom of the day, which often
mistook various medical conditions for demon possession.
Matthew 4:24, however, makes a clear distinction between
those "who were ill with various diseases" and those who
were "demon-possessed."

The Bible describes some of the symptoms that often
went with demon possession. When a father pleaded with
Jesus to heal his demon-possessed son, he told Jesus that
the "spirit seizes him and he suddenly screams; it throws
him into convulsions so that he foams at the mouth. It
scarcely ever leaves him and is destroying him" (Luke
9:39). Mark 9:22 adds that this destructive behavior
included throwing him into fire and water to kill him.
Other physical signs include a loss of speech and sight
(Matthew 12:22). In Luke 13:11 we read about a woman
who "had been crippled by a spirit."

Another thing that would set demon possession apart
from a medical condition is the way the possessed reacted
to Jesus. The evil spirit would often recognize Jesus as the

Son of God and Savior of the world. He would acknowledge him whose will he was forced to obey. This shows the truth of James 2:19, which says that the demons shudder at the thought of God.

From the Bible we see that multiple possession is also possible. Mary Magdalene was possessed by seven demons (Luke 8:2). When Jesus questioned the spirit who possessed the Gerasene man, he was told, "My name is Legion . . . for we are many" (Mark 5:9). It is also possible that the man who shouted at Jesus in the synagogue in Capernaum was suffering from multiple possession. Using the plural he asked Jesus, "What do you want with us, Jesus of Nazareth? Have you come to destroy us? I know who you are—the Holy One of God!" (Luke 4:34). Whether this indicates multiple possession or whether the demon is using the collective *we* isn't clear. One person who has studied some recent cases of demon possession notes that evil spirits often use the singular and plural pronouns interchangeably. "When it speaks, it will sometimes refer to itself as 'I' and sometimes as 'we,' will use 'my' and 'our.'"[32]

The demon-possessed today

The Bible clearly teaches that demon possession is real. But was it something unique to Jesus' time? Or does it still happen today? If so, how commonly does it occur? A study of the evidence would indicate that demon possession does still happen today, although it is rare, especially compared to Jesus' time, when it seemed to be fairly common. A Lutheran pastor who counsels with victims of demon possession states that he has dealt with some 50 cases during his 20-year ministry. When we take into account that his referrals come from a large metropolitan area and span many years, we see that demon possession is far from a common occurrence.

When we look at the background of the demon-possessed, similar circumstances are often evident. Some have been involved with satanic activity, such as devil worship, witchcraft, divination, Ouija boards, or other forms of the occult. They walked into the devil's cage and the "lion" sank his teeth into their lives.

Another common thread is an unrepented sin that stands out in the person's life. In this way the person may have given the devil a foothold (Ephesians 4:27). For Judas Iscariot the open door was a love for money. For Ananias and Sapphira deceit and a desire for the approval of others caused Satan to fill their hearts (Acts 5:3). Whether they were actually possessed isn't clear from the biblical account. Most likely they were not. Yet in both cases the devil led them away from God and into deadly sin.

A final factor that often leads to demon possession is generational involvement in the occult. Perhaps a parent, grandparent, or other relative was heavily involved in worshiping the devil or practicing his evil arts. The devil may use this generational tie to lay claim to a person's body and soul.

As Christians we can be confident that we are God's children and have been redeemed with the blood of Christ. We might think of the words that are commonly spoken in the cemetery during a Christian committal service: "May God the Father who has created this body, may God the Son who by His blood has redeemed this body together with the soul, may God the Holy Spirit who by Baptism has sanctified this body to be His temple, keep these remains unto the day of the resurrection of all flesh."[33] This blessing echoes the words of Romans 14:8: "If we live, we live to the Lord; and if we die, we die to the Lord. So, whether we live or die, we belong to the Lord." As children of God, the devil can lay no claim to our bodies and souls. Through faith in the crucified Christ, we belong to the Lord.

But how can we know whether or not we are dealing with an actual case of demon possession? What are some of the symptoms? When confronted with a case of possible demon possession, one has to be careful to rule out all other causes for the condition. It is likely that many who were considered demon-possessed in past centuries and even many who are thought to be possessed today actually suffer from a mental or physical disease. Some medical conditions display symptoms that closely resemble demon possession. Those who deal with demon possession are careful to rule out every physical cause for the person's behavior before proceeding with counseling. The Lutheran minister mentioned earlier has an elaborate checklist he fills out on each person. This helps him determine whether demon possession is likely in a particular case.

Certain distinct signs set demon possession apart as a unique phenomenon. Some are evident in the person who is possessed. They include levitation (the possessed person may rise and float in the air); possessed gravity (the possessed person becomes immovable); a change in personality, voice, or physical appearance; the ability to speak other languages not known to the possessed person; superhuman strength; supernatural knowledge of things in the past or present; extremely foul language or lifestyle; violent behavior; and an obvious aversion to Christ and Christian symbols. Sometimes any Christian symbol will be hidden from sight, proving that the aversion is demonic and not psychological. Many who work with the possessed consider an aversion to Christ or Christian symbols as the most striking sign of possession. This would agree with biblical accounts. Both during the ministry of Christ and in the early church, demon-possessed people would recognize Christ or one of his apostles, often in a vocal and violent manner.

The signs of demon possession, however, are not only seen in the person who is possessed. They may also be evident in the place where the possessed person is situated. These may include an overwhelming stench, freezing or extremely hot temperatures, objects flying around the room, wallpaper peeling off the wall, strange noises, tearing of fabric, violent smashing of furniture or glass items, lights turning on by themselves even when unplugged, objects appearing in places where they were not put, and the constant opening and slamming of doors. Obviously these are symptoms that no physical or psychological disorder could cause. We might also note that not all these signs will be evident in every case of demon possession. And usually the signs of possession are not as dramatic as those shown in occult movies. Initially one may wonder if it was a freak of nature or whether such things were simply imagined. Only after these things happen repeatedly does one begin to realize that other forces may be at work.

Besides possessing people, demons may also possess places. In fact, it seems that evil spirits want to possess some person or area, even though as spirits they occupy no physical space. This was true of the many spirits that possessed the Gerasene man. When Jesus commanded them to leave the man, they pleaded, "Send us among the pigs; allow us to go into them" (Mark 5:12). Malachi Martin reports this same phenomenon. In his study of exorcism he has found that "one aspect of possession and of spirit makes itself apparent: the close connection between spirit and physical location. . . . That there is some connection between spirit and place must be dealt with as a fact."[34]

The space that a demon possesses may be a human body. Or it may be a house or other building. While we have to be careful about believing every haunted house story that is reported, various poltergeist phenomena and paranormal activities have been documented. We have no reason to doubt that these things may be due to the devil.

The Roman rite of exorcism

The Roman Catholic Church is one of only a few churches that has a formal rite of exorcism. In recent years, however, church leaders have used this rite very sparingly, not only because of the sensationalism that goes with the subject, but also because other approaches are often used with the possessed. Father James J. LeBar is a Roman Catholic priest who assists with exorcisms in New York City. In a phone conversation with the author, LeBar indicated that in his diocese they perform about one exorcism a year. He also stated that besides New York City, he knows of only one other place in the United States where the Roman Catholic Church performs exorcisms.

At first glance, one will notice that Roman Catholic exorcisms are quite different from those performed by Jesus and the apostles. Exorcisms often take hours, even days, before a demon-possessed person is delivered and include rituals and rites lacking in biblical accounts. The process seems to be a contest of wills between the demon and the one trying to cast it out. Using the Wild West analogy, one is reminded of a gun fight, which matches the skills of one against the other.

Besides the rite of exorcism, the Roman Catholic Church also uses other methods to deal with demon possession. Some Roman Catholics, especially those with charismatic leanings, rely on prayer deliverance. Other segments of the Roman Church employ more tradi-tional methods of counseling to deal with those who are afflicted.

The possessor

The Bible paints an ugly picture of Satan and his band of outlaws. In Revelation 9 their evil efforts are compared to locusts devouring the earth. The pain they inflict on the unbelieving people of the world is like that of a scor-pion when it strikes a man. A few chapters later, Satan is pictured as an enormous red dragon with seven heads and ten horns (12:3). These pictures are enough to let us know that the devil and his demons are thoroughly evil.

This truth is reinforced by those who have come face to face with demon possession. They describe it as being in the presence of pure evil. Martin states that during an exorcism the priest "is made to know he is touching the completely unclean, the totally unhuman."[35]

In demon possession Satan's accuser role becomes clear. He may confront people with many of their secret sins. He will use these in an effort to break down even the strongest person and lead him or her to despair. When faced with demon possession, one has to exercise extreme care lest he be overcome by these "flaming arrows of the evil one" (Ephesians 6:16).

The story behind The Exorcist

A well-documented case of demon possession and exor-cism occurred in St. Louis, Missouri, in 1949. It involved a 14-year-old boy named Douglas Deen, whose story became the basis for the movie The Exorcist.[36]

Even though Deen had an ordinary childhood, he was especially close to a spiritist aunt who introduced him to the Ouija board. Following her death, the young teenager became obsessed with playing the board. Soon his family heard strange sounds in their home, especially in the boy's bedroom. It started with a dripping sound and then a scratching noise. Soon more bizarre things began to happen. Chairs would flip over, and objects would move across the room. Then it became clear that an evil spirit had taken control of the boy's body. It tormented him night after night. No sooner did Deen settle in for the night when his bed began shaking. In desperation the family finally turned to a Roman Catholic priest who, after numerous lengthy sessions, was able to exorcise the demon.

Dealing with demon possession

What if we are faced with a case of demon possession? How should we deal with the situation? Nowhere does the Bible give us a formula for casting out evil spirits. Nor does the Lord promise us the power to expel demons in a manner similar to what was practiced in the time of Jesus and the apostles. That may very well have been a special gift similar to the ability to heal and perform other miracles.

The most effective weapons in this area are God's Word and prayer. James 5:16 assures us "the prayer of a righteous man is powerful and effective." Jesus also promises that he will give us whatever we ask the Father in his name (John 16:23).

Together with prayer goes the Word of God. A Lutheran minister explains, "In counseling with the troubled person, I point out again and again that he or she is a redeemed child of God and that the demon has no right to that person's body." When we recall that Jesus used God's Word to drive off the devil and resist his temptations, we see that God's Word is still the most effective weapon in dealing with demon possession. As Martin Luther wrote in his most famous hymn, "One little word can fell him" (CW 200:3). When we confront the devil with "the sword of the Spirit, which is the word of God" (Ephesians 6:17), his only option is to get out of town as fast as he can.

If you suspect that someone close to you is demon-possessed, consult with your pastor. If he does not feel equipped to counsel the person, he would be able to refer you to someone who is. Remember, Jesus died for all. Therefore Satan can lay claim to no one.

8

Satanism

Idolizing the Outlaw

Some of the villains of the Wild West were regarded as heroes in their time. One such person was Sam Bass. He led a band of bank and train robbers. Because he stole from the rich and gave to the poor, he became known as the Robin Hood of Texas. Following his death at age 27, his legend was kept alive by a ballad that bears his name and also by stories about his generosity to the poor. Even though he was an outlaw, he became known as a "good" bad guy.

This is what some do with the devil. They not only follow his ways; they actually idolize him as a hero and worship him as a god. Their practice is called Satanism, and it is one of the ugliest and crassest sins against the First Commandment. For these people idolize the greatest outlaw, Satan.

Most-wanted list

When a notorious outlaw went on a crime spree, a wanted poster was often hung, calling for his arrest. Besides showing a picture of the outlaw, these posters would say something about his crimes. They might also warn people that the outlaw was armed and dangerous.

Satanism also has its outlaws. One of the most infamous was Aleister Crowley. Born in England in 1875, Crowley had the benefit of a Christian home. His parents were Plymouth Brethren who took their faith seriously. His father, a wealthy retired brewer, spent much of his time spreading the Word.

Even though Crowley had great respect for his father, he came to loathe the Christian faith. At an early age he was fascinated by the occult. He grew so devious that his own mother referred to him as "The Beast," after the creature described in Revelation. Crowley willingly accepted this name and did his best to live up to the reputation.

While on a trip to Egypt, Crowley claimed he was contacted by a spirit he later called Aiwass. This spirit dictated to him *The Book of the Law*, which proclaimed the coming of a new age. It also set down this principle: Do what thou wilt shall be the whole of the law. His life of witchcraft, drug abuse, homosexuality, fornication, and other forms of perversion shows that he lived by this principle. More than anyone else, Crowley's life and writings have had a strong influence on Satanism in America.

Four kinds—one crime

Modern Satanists can be divided into four groups: (1) dabblers or experimentalists, (2) self-styled Satanists, (3) members of public satanic churches, and (4) generational Satanists.[37]

Dabblers and experimentalists most often consist of young people ages 11 through 19. They often come from middle- to upper-class families and have an above-average intelligence. They become interested in the occult through heavy metal music, movies with occult themes, or fantasy and role-playing games. Many are at a transitional time in their lives—they are just entering high school or college or have experienced a loss in their lives.

The term *self-styled Satanist* is usually applied to those involved in criminal activity. They use the age-old argument "The devil made me do it!" as a rationale for their crimes. Richard Ramirez, the "Night Stalker," would be an example of a self-styled Satanist. While on trial for several murders in southern California in the mid 1980s, he held up his hand for all to see a satanic symbol inscribed on his palm.

Members of public satanic churches and generational Satanists are less visible than the other two groups. They have a more organized structure and often have a cult "royalty," which passes teachings from one generation to the next.

Studies have revealed that many of those who turn to Satanism are from troubled homes. This not only applies to dabblers but also those who join satanic cults. When young people don't find support and acceptance in a loving, Christian home, they often search for it elsewhere. Many become easy prey for the devil.

This observation will concern us as Christians, especially when we see Christian families fracturing. It points out the need for strong Christian leadership on the part of parents. Joshua's words to the people of Israel are still a good motto for Christian homes: "As for me and my household, we will serve the LORD" (Joshua 24:15).

Satan wants you!

The main outlaw in modern Satanism in America is Anton LaVey. Often called the "black pope," LaVey left school at age 16 and joined the Clyde Beatty Circus, where he worked as a cage boy and then as an assistant lion tamer. At 18 he left the circus to play the organ for carnivals and tent-show evangelists. Obviously, this contact with the seedier side of society affected his attitude toward human nature and God. In his introduction to *The Satanic Bible* he states:

> I would see men lusting after half-naked girls dancing at the carnival, and on Sunday morning when I was playing the organ for tent-show evangelists at the other end of the carnival lot, I would see these same men sitting in the pews with their wives and children, asking God to forgive them and purge them of carnal desires. And the next Saturday night they'd be back at the carnival or some other place of indulgence. I knew then that the Christian church thrives on hypocrisy, and that man's carnal nature will win out.[38]

His later job as a photographer for the San Francisco Police Department only reinforced these beliefs. He adds: "I saw the bloodiest, grimiest side of human nature. It was disgusting and depressing."[39] This, together with his interest in the occult, led him into Satanism.

On Walpurgisnacht (the eve of May Day), April 30, 1966, LaVey formed the Magic Circle, which soon became the Church of Satan. With the help of certain media events, this group received almost immediate recognition. These events included a satanic wedding and funeral as well as the satanic baptism of LaVey's three-year-old daughter. Another big boost came when LaVey served as a consultant and even played the role of the devil in the 1960s movie *Rosemary's Baby*. LaVey himself called this movie "the best paid commercial for Satanism since the Inquisition."[40]

In an effort to recruit others to his cause, this outlaw began circulating a wanted poster of his own. It showed a picture of LaVey dressed up like a satanic Uncle Sam with the slogan "Satan Wants You!"

This publicity brought a sudden influx of members, among them Hollywood celebrities such as Sammy Davis Jr. and sex symbol Jayne Mansfeld. The latter was especially close to LaVey, and her untimely death in a car accident left him shaken. Apparently he had put a curse on her lawyer and lover, Sam Brody, who was driving the car and was also killed in the accident.

By 1970 the Church of Satan had groups called "grottos" in almost every major city in America. Its membership numbered in the thousands. But with this sudden growth came significant problems, many of them involving power and personality struggles between LaVey and his followers. Soon many of the grottos were closed, and the leader changed his recruitment strategy from that of the Army to that of the Marines. He was now looking for a "few good men."

This internal strife that LaVey's Church of Satan experienced shouldn't surprise us. Sin has taken its toll on the Christian church, resulting in many different denominations. It continues to cause conflicts in God's church and often hinders his work. How much more won't it happen in a group where sin has no limits and where self-indulgence is given free reign?

The breakup of LaVey's gang led to the formation of many other smaller satanic groups, one of the more prominent ones being the Temple of Set formed by Michael Aquino. As a lieutenant in the Army, Aquino first met LaVey in 1969. He was soon promoted to general in LaVey's army, where he was ordained a priest of Satan. For several years he served as LaVey's right-hand man in the Church of Satan. By 1972 a power struggle between the two caused Aquino to leave the Church of Satan and form the Temple of Set—the Egyptian name for Satan. Some put the number of satanic groups in the United States in the hundreds. While this number may be somewhat exaggerated, most are small groups centered around a local leader.

Even though LaVey is not as visible as he once was, he is still actively pursuing his evil ways. Besides producing a number of newsletters, he is also represented on the World Wide Web, together with a Twin Cities group called Satan's PlayGround Grotto. Established in 1994, this daughter congregation has as its stated goal to bring satanic awareness to the Minnesota area. Of special interest is the e-mail address for this Minnesota grotto. It is spelled "Baalack" and seems to be a combination of the word *Baal,* a common Old Testament idol, and the color *black.* Possibly this word also incorporates the name Balak, the wicked king of Moab who asked Balaam to put a curse on God's people of Israel (Numbers 22). All these are a fitting representation for Satan's church.

LaVey's legacy—The Satanic Bible

Outlaws often leave a legacy. It may come in the form of a song or legend that glorifies their deeds and inspires others to follow in their footsteps. LaVey has also left a legacy—*The Satanic Bible*. Published in 1969, it has sold over a million copies.

Unlike some Satanists, LaVey denies that the devil is a real being. He considers Satan symbolic of self-indulgence and sin. It is interesting that the father of lies can even lead his followers to believe one of the greatest lies of all—that the devil doesn't exist. LaVey's belief that Satan merely represents everything evil is reflected in the Nine Satanic Statements. As a parody of the Ten Commandments they state:

1. Satan represents indulgence instead of abstinence.

2. Satan represents vital existence instead of spiritual pipe dreams.

3. Satan represents undefiled wisdom instead of hypocritical self-deceit.

4. Satan represents kindness to those who deserve it instead of love wasted on ingrates.

5. Satan represents vengeance instead of turning the other cheek.

6. Satan represents responsibility to the responsible instead of concern for psychic vampires.

7. Satan represents man as just another animal, sometimes better, more often worse than those that walk on all fours, who because of his "divine spiritual and intellectual development" has become the most vicious animal of all.

8. Satan represents all of the so-called sins, as they all lead to physical, mental, or emotional gratification.

9. Satan has been the best friend the church has ever had, as he has kept it in business all these years.[41]

Besides listing the Nine Satanic Statements, *The Satanic Bible* has four major parts. The Book of Satan (Fire) has five chapters that mimic and mock God's Word. While one is reluctant to repeat such sacrilegious statements, perhaps a few will help us understand LaVey's extreme depravity. In an effort to mock the crucifixion account he states, "I dip my forefinger in the watery blood of your impotent mad redeemer, and write over his thorn-torn brow: The TRUE prince of evil—the king of all slaves" (Chapter 1:6).[42] Chapter 2 opens with this question: "Behold the crucifix; what does it symbolize? Pallid incompetence hanging on a tree" (Chapter 2:1).[43] His attack on the Easter message reads like this: "There is no heaven of glory bright, and no hell where sinners roast . . . no redeemer liveth" (Chapter 4:2).[44] The final chapter is a mockery of the Beatitudes. LaVey writes, "Blessed are those that believe in what is best for them, for never shall their minds be terrorized—Cursed are the 'lambs of God,' for they shall be bled whiter than snow" (Chapter 5:9).[45] Chapter 4:3 echoes the age-old lie of the devil that is at the heart of Satanism: "Say unto thine own heart, 'I am mine own redeemer.'"[46]

The second part of *The Satanic Bible* is called The Book of Lucifer (Air), which explains some of the Nine Satanic Statements. This is followed by The Book of Belial (Earth), which describes the practice, paraphernalia, and rituals of Satanism. The final book, The Book of Leviathan (Water), lists traditional invocations to the devil, which are used during satanic ritual.

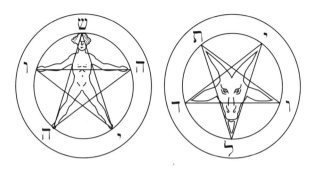

Upright and inverted pentagram

The upright pentagram on the left is usually a symbol of witchcraft. It represents the human body and the power it receives from the earth.

Satanism usually uses the inverted pentagram pictured on the right. In the parable of the sheep and the goats (Matthew 25:31-46), Jesus pictures the unbelievers as goats. Thus a goat's head is used as a symbol for Satan.

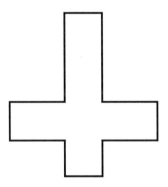

Upside-down cross

Just as the cross represents Christ's victory over death on Calvary, so the inverted cross represents the defeat of Christianity.

The number 666
The number given to the devil in Revelation 13:18.

Cross of confusion
This symbol combines the cross with a question mark. The implications seem obvious—it questions the validity of Christ.

Lightning bolt

In Luke 10:18 Jesus states, "I saw Satan fall like lightning from heaven." Satanists often use the lightning bolt as a power symbol.

Nine Satanic Statements symbol

This symbol appears in *The Satanic Bible* together with the Nine Satanic Statements.

Anarchy symbol

This symbol represents the abolition of all law. It is widely used by heavy metal music fans and those who dabble in Satanism.

Diana and Lucifer

The crescent moon and the star are common symbols in witchcraft and Satanism. They represent Diana, the moon goddess, and Lucifer, the morning star.

To *The Satanic Bible* LaVey has also added *The Satanic Rituals*, a how-to guide for Satanists. It contains many of the ceremonies LaVey has adapted from ancient rites, as well as suggestions for local groups to concoct their own.

LaVey's most recent addition is *The Devil's Notebook*. It was written in 1992 and discusses a number of topics, including nonconformity and occult faddism.

When we look at the life and times of outlaw LaVey, we can only conclude that he is one of the people Jude speaks about when he says, "They are wild waves of the sea, foaming up their shame; wandering stars, for whom blackest darkness has been reserved forever" (Jude 13).

The Black Mass

A common ceremony in Satan worship is the Black Mass. Since Satanism was usually practiced behind the scenes, the origin of this satanic rite is unknown. Some trace it back as far as the Council of Toledo, held in 681. This council banned the so-called Mass of the Dead, which was performed to secure someone's death.

Elements of the Black Mass also appear in the trial of Lady Alice Kyteler in Ireland in 1324. The charges against her included "defiling certain holy objects used in Holy Communion."[47]

Another reference to the Black Mass involves a scandal that took place in France during the reign of Louis XIV. While investigating some poisonings in the royal family, authorities discovered that some within the king's court had regularly sought help from a high priestess of Satan. As the plot unfolded, the woman confessed she had sacrificed over 2,500 infants in her satanic ceremonies, including the Black Mass.

The repulsive rituals of the Black Mass vary by time and place. The altar is usually the naked body of a woman. On the altar is an upside-down cross. The elements include wine mixed with blood or urine and a wafer that may be laced with drugs. Everything is done to ridicule the Lord's Supper and break down the inhibitions of those who attend. The whole ceremony often ends with a sexual orgy. A more blasphemous mockery of the Lord's Supper is hardly imaginable! It goes without saying that those who partake of this spiritual perversion eat and drink judgment on themselves.

The Christian Lord's Supper

By contrast, what a precious gift our Lord Jesus has given us Christians in his own New Testament Supper!

From God's Word we recognize the many blessings God gives in the Lord's Supper. Some are deeply personal. This would include the special, personal assurance that our sins are forgiven. Although God gives this same assurance through his Word and also through Holy Baptism, the Lord's Supper is different. We might compare it to a birthday card or gift. Just as a card or gift is a special way of wishing someone a happy birthday, so the Lord's Supper is a special way in which God tells us, "I love you, and I forgive your sins for the sake of my Son." The more times and the more different ways God tells us this gospel message, the more we will believe it. Thus the Lord's Supper also strengthens our faith—another personal blessing.

This sacrament is also a part of public worship. Thus it includes blessings we share with others. One is the opportunity to confess our faith. Paul tells us, "Whenever you eat this bread and drink this cup, you proclaim the Lord's death until he comes" (1 Corinthians 11:26). Jesus told his disciples, "Do this in remembrance of me" (Luke 22:19). When we observe the Lord's Supper, we are making a confession of faith to others. Jesus stressed the importance of confessing our faith when he said, "Whoever acknowledges me before men, I will also acknowledge him before my Father in heaven" (Matthew 10:32). The apostle Paul told the Romans, "It is with your mouth that you confess and are saved" (10:10). The Lord's Supper gives us a unique opportunity to confess our faith to fellow Christians.

And it also gives us an opportunity to confess our faith with fellow Christians. Paul told the Corinthians, "We, who are many, are one body, for we all partake of the one loaf" (1 Corinthians 10:17). We are not only one with God in this Sacrament; we are also one with our fellow Christians. We express our unity of faith when we commune together.

When we remember the many blessings the Lord gives us in this Sacrament, certainly we will want to receive it regularly. This will help us resist the attacks of Satan and his evil band of outlaws.

9

The Defeat of Satan

How Our Rest Was Won

Perhaps you have seen the movie classic *How the West Was Won*. It shows some of the struggles and hardships early settlers faced as they moved west. Scripture shows us a similar scene. But instead of being called *How the West Was Won*, this one might be called *How Our Rest Was Won*. It deals with the eternal rest we will enjoy in heaven and shows how the battle for our salvation was fought and won.

The day Jesus rode into town

It's a common scene in westerns. A lonely stranger strides into town. As he does, the people of the town stop and stare. Some gaze out their windows. Others stand in the doorways of their shops or businesses and watch as the stranger passes by. It's as if the whole town is captivated and paralyzed by the sight of the stranger on the horse. They all want to know who he is and where he comes from. They all want to know why he has come to town.

The situation was quite different the day Jesus rode into town. When he entered Jerusalem on Palm Sunday, people didn't stop and stare. They didn't give him a cold shoulder. They received him with open arms and gave him a hero's welcome. Matthew 21:8,9 tells us: "A very large crowd spread their cloaks on the road, while others cut branches from the trees and spread them on the road. The crowds that went ahead of him and those that followed shouted, 'Hosanna to the Son of David!' 'Blessed is he who comes in the name of the Lord!' 'Hosanna in the highest!'"

At first it didn't seem as though Jesus was coming in humility. It seemed more like a celebration. Everything looked glorious until we see what Jesus was riding—a donkey. This was hardly the kind of animal a hero in the Wild West would ride into town. If he did, he would be laughed out of town in no time at all. Yet that's what Jesus was riding the day he rode into town.

This reflected his humility in coming to earth. It stressed the truth that "the Son of Man did not come to be served, but to serve, and to give his life as a ransom for many" (Mark 10:45). Even though Jesus was the Sheriff of heaven and earth, he didn't go around flashing his badge. He didn't dress in full uniform in order to demand the respect of everyone he met. He dressed like a servant and wore the clothes of humility.

David describes Jesus' humility in Psalm 8. He states: "What is man that you are mindful of him, the son of man that you care for him? You made him a little lower than the heavenly beings and crowned him with glory and honor" (verses 4,5). These words apply first to our creation as human beings. God made us a little lower than the angels. Yet these words also apply to the Son of Man— Jesus Christ. By humbling himself, Jesus became a little lower than the heavenly beings. This was demonstrated several times during his ministry. Following his temptation in the wilderness (Matthew 4:11) and also after he prayed in Gethsemane (Luke 22:43), the Bible tells us angels came and attended him. In humility Jesus received help from these heavenly beings.

But Jesus didn't humble himself for no reason at all. He did it to carry out an important mission. The reason why he rode into town was to defeat and capture Satan and his gang of outlaws. First John 3:8 tells us, "The reason the Son of God appeared was to destroy the devil's work." Hebrews 2:14,15 also spells out Jesus' mission in coming to earth: "Since the children have flesh and blood, he too shared in their humanity so that by his death he might destroy him who holds the power of death—that is, the devil—and free those who all their lives were held in slavery by their fear of death."

One of the most notorious outlaws of the Wild West was Jesse James. Together with his brother, Frank, and the rest of the James Gang, he terrorized the country in the 1800s. Their illegal escapades lasted over a decade and brought them as far north as Minnesota in the famous and infamous attempt to rob a bank in Northfield, Minnesota.

That's what the devil and his gang are like. They have been terrorizing the world ever since they outwitted Adam and Eve in the Garden of Eden. They have gone on a rampage similar to that of Jesse James. But instead of robbing banks, Satan and his gang steal souls. They rob people of hope in life and confidence in death. As a result, their faces appear on God's wanted posters in heaven. And because of all the damage they have done, they aren't wanted dead or alive. They are wanted more dead than alive.

The day Jesus rode into town, he had one thing on his mind. He had come to get the notorious outlaw Satan. He was determined to gun him down in the greatest gunfight of all time. This was reflected in the name Jesus was given on Palm Sunday. He was called the Son of David. This name acknowledged him to be the Messiah, the hero who would stop Satan in his tracks and end his reign of terror. "Son of David" identified Jesus as the long arm of the law, who would bring justice to the earth. It identified him as the seed of the woman God had promised to send (Genesis 3:15).

But even though Jesus represented the law, the leaders of the day treated him more like an outlaw. When he came riding into town that Palm Sunday, they smelled trouble. They had sold themselves over to Satan a long time ago. And they didn't take too kindly to some stranger coming in and cleaning up the town. They were happy with the situation just as it was. So they set up a plot to get rid of Jesus. They formed a lynching party, and within days they had Jesus strung up on a tree. For a time it looked as though the bad guys had won. It looked as though Satan's reign of terror would continue and that Jesus had suffered a humiliating defeat at the hands of Satan's gang.

The shoot-out at the Calvary Corral

The important thing isn't how you ride into town. What counts is how you ride out. This was especially true in the case of Christ. He may have come in humility, but he left in glory.

The most famous gunfight is probably the shoot-out at the O. K. Corral in Tombstone, Arizona. It featured one of the most famous lawmen in the history of the Wild West—Wyatt Earp. This shoot-out lasted only 60 seconds, but when the dust had cleared, everyone was either dead or wounded except for the hero—Wyatt Earp. He walked away without a scratch.

The most famous spiritual gunfight of all time took place at the "Calvary Corral." The results were similar to what happened at the O. K. Corral. For when the dust of Calvary had cleared and the sun rose on Easter Sunday, only one man was left standing—the Son of Man. The devil had been gunned down. He took a bullet to the head, which crushed his skull and dropped him on the spot. The rest of his gang—the Jewish leaders—were wounded. They were at a loss for words. The very man they had hung on a tree was now back in the saddle. He had managed to escape the most secure prison there is—the grave. No longer was Jesus riding a lowly donkey. Now he was riding a white horse. Even though Jesus rode into town in humility, he was clearly riding out in glory. Hanging over the back of his horse was the body, bound hand and foot, of the notorious outlaw called Satan. The apostle John pictures this victory in vivid terms in Revelation 20:2,3. In speaking about Jesus he states: "He seized the dragon, that ancient serpent, who is the devil, or Satan, and bound him for a thousand years. He threw him into the Abyss, and locked and sealed it over him, to keep him from deceiving the nations anymore."

Riding off into the sunset

This, then, is the story of how our rest was won. And as we can see, we can't take credit for the hope of heaven we have. For we too have lived a life of crime. We also deserve to be on God's wanted poster. We deserve to be strung up for our sins and sentenced to serve time in Satan's prison. Yet Jesus planned an amazing escape. Through his perfect life he slipped us the key to the prison cell. Through his willing death he secured our safe release. Because of what Jesus did, we join the psalm writer in saying, "O LORD, our Lord, how majestic is your name in all the earth!" (Psalm 8:1).

And when Jesus returns on the Last Day to rescue us from this world, he will do so in glory. When he comes to town at the end of time, he won't be riding a donkey; he will be mounted on a white horse. The apostle John gives us a preview of this glorious event when he says:

> I saw heaven standing open and there before me was a white horse, whose rider is called Faithful and True. With justice he judges and makes war. His eyes are like blazing fire, and on his head are many crowns. He has a name written on him that no one knows but he himself. He is dressed in a robe dipped in blood, and his name is the Word of God. The armies of heaven were following him, riding on white horses and dressed in fine linen, white and clean. Out of his mouth comes a sharp sword with which to strike down the nations. "He will rule them with an iron scepter." He treads the winepress of the fury of the wrath of God Almighty. On his robe and on his thigh he has this name written: KING OF KINGS AND LORD OF LORDS (Revelation 19:11-16).

Every year Hollywood hands out Oscar awards. Judges decide which is the best picture of the year and who is the best actor or actress. If God would hand out an Oscar for best picture, there's no doubt which one would win. It would be the movie *How Our Rest Was Won*. God himself has clearly earned all the honors as best director in planning and executing this story of our salvation. And there would be no doubt who would win best actor. It would go to the star of the show—Jesus Christ. In a classic battle of good versus evil, Jesus came in humility but left in glory. And because of what Jesus did, we know our story will also have a happy ending. When Jesus returns in glory at the end of time, we won't be left standing and staring. Christ will come to take us home. Together with our victorious hero, Jesus Christ, we will ride off into the sunset of eternal glory.

Endnotes

[1]Apology of the Augsburg Confession, Article XXI:8, *The Book of Concord: The Confessions of the Evangelical Lutheran Church,* translated and edited by Theodore G. Tappert (Philadelphia: Fortress Press, 1959), p. 230.

[2]Malachi Martin, *Hostage to the Devil* (New York: Reader's Digest Press, 1976), p. 19.

[3]Louise Lague, Leah Feldon-Mitchell, Moira Bailey, and Ellin Stein, "Spheres of Influence," *People Weekly* (October 24, 1994), p. 88.

[4]Lague et al., "Spheres of Influence," p. 86.

[5]Laurence Zuckerman, "The First Lady's Astrologer," *Time* (May 16, 1988), p. 41.

[6]Siegbert W. Becker, *Wizards That Peep* (Milwaukee: Northwestern Publishing House, 1978), p. 11.

[7]Lague et al., "Spheres of Influence," p. 91.

[8]Jeane Dixon, "Your Horoscope," *Winona Daily News* (September 1, 1995), p. 9A, cols. 1,2.

[9]Joan Hake Robie, *The Truth About Dungeons & Dragons* (Lancaster, Pa.: Starburst Publishers, 1991), pp. 46,47.

[10]Jerry Johnson, *The Edge of Evil* (Dallas: Word Publishing, 1989), p. 106.

[11]Stoker Hunt, *Ouija—The Most Dangerous Game* (New York: Harper and Row, 1976), p. 6.

[12]Hunt, *Ouija*, p. 89.

[13]Quoted from the video *Rock and the Christian's Role*, produced by the WELS Commission on Youth Discipleship.

[14]Quoted from the video *Learn to Discern: Help for a Generation at Risk*, produced by Focus on the Family, 1992.

[15]Selena Fox, "Introduction to the Wiccan Religion and Contemporary Paganism," (Mount Horeb, Wis.: Circle Sanctuary, 1994). This sheet was sent to the author when he requested information on witchcraft from Circle Sanctuary.

[16]Fox, "Introduction."

[17]James J. LeBar, *Cults, Sects, and the New Age* (Huntington, Ind.: Our Sunday Visitor Publishing Division, 1989), p. 162.

[18]Fox, "Introduction."

[19]Raymond Buckland, *Witchcraft from the Inside* (St. Paul: Llewellyn Publications, 1995), p. 106.

[20]Shaune Ralph, "I Am Not a Wicked Witch," *Mademoiselle* (June 1994), p. 144.

[21]Fox, "Introduction."

[22]Fox, "Introduction."

[23]Taken from "A Pledge to Pagan Spirituality" by Pagan Spirit Alliance, a special Pagan friendship network within Circle Sanctuary.

[24]Ruth A. Tucker, *Another Gospel* (Grand Rapids: Zondervan Publishing House, 1989), p. 320.

[25]Tucker, *Another Gospel*, p. 321.

[26]Douglas R. Groothuis, *Unmasking the New Age* (Downers Grove, Ill.: Intervarsity Press, 1986), pp. 18-31.

[27]Groothuis, *Unmasking*, p. 18.

[28]Groothuis, *Unmasking*, p. 21.

[29]Tucker, *Another Gospel*, p. 333.

[30]Tucker, *Another Gospel*, p. 332.

[31]LeBar, *Cults*, p. 135.

[32]Martin, *Hostage*, p. 18.

[33]WELS, *The Pastor's Agenda* (Milwaukee: Northwestern Publishing House, 1990), p. 31.

[34]Martin, *Hostage*, p. 14.

[35]Martin, *Hostage*, p. 23.

[36]Thomas B. Allen, *Possessed—The True Story of an Exorcism* (New York: Doubleday, 1993). The various signs of demon possession mentioned in Chapter 7 are recorded in this book.

[37]Joan Hickey, "Pastoral Responses to the Phenomenon of Satanism in America Today," *Catholic Theological Union*, Vol. 4, No. 3 (August 1991), p. 16.

[38]Anton Szandor LaVey, *The Satanic Bible* (New York: Avon Books, 1969), p. 12.

[39]LaVey, *The Satanic Bible*, p. 13.

[40]Bruce G. Frederickson, *How to Respond to Satanism* (St. Louis: Concordia Publishing House, 1988), p. 17.

[41]LaVey, *The Satanic Bible*, p. 25.

[42]LaVey, *The Satanic Bible*, p. 31.

[43]LaVey, *The Satanic Bible*, p. 31.

[44]LaVey, *The Satanic Bible*, p. 33.

[45]LaVey, *The Satanic Bible*, p. 34.

[46]LaVey, *The Satanic Bible*, p. 33.

[47]Frederickson, *How to Respond*, p. 14.

For Further Reading

Becker, Siegbert W. *Wizards That Peep*. Milwaukee: Northwestern Publishing House, 1978.

Hoenecke, Roland. "The Angels—Agents of Preservation," in *Our Great Heritage*, Vol. 2. Edited by Lyle W. Lange. Milwaukee: Northwestern Publishing House, 1991.

Jahn, Richard C. "The Doctrine of the Angels," in *The Abiding Word*, Vol. 3. St. Louis: Concordia Publishing House, 1960.

Vogel, Heinrich J. "The Angel of the Lord," *Wisconsin Lutheran Quarterly*, Vol. 73, No. 2 (April 1976).

Warnke, Richard E. *The Angels: Mighty Servants of God*. Milwaukee: Northwestern Publishing House, 1987.

Scripture Index

128   ANGELS AND DEMONS

Subject Index